Where
Is God
When Bad
Things Happen?

D0067540

**Walnut Hill
Church Library
Bethel, CT 06801**

Where Is God When Bad Things Happen?

FINDING SOLACE IN
TIMES OF TROUBLE

LUIS PALAU
WITH STEVE HALLIDAY

GALILEE
DOUBLEDAY
New York London Toronto Sydney Auckland

Walnut Hill
Church Library
Bethel, CT 06801

248·86
Pal

A GALILEE BOOK
PUBLISHED BY DOUBLEDAY
a division of Random House, Inc.
1540 Broadway, New York, New York 10036

GALILEE, DOUBLEDAY, and the portrayal of a ship with a cross above a book are trademarks of Doubleday, a division of Random House, Inc.

First Galilee edition published June 2000 by special arrangement with Doubleday.

Book design by Bonni Leon-Berman.

All references are from the *Holy Bible: New International Version*, copyright © 1973, 1978, 1984 by the International Bible Society.

The Library of Congress has cataloged the 1999 Doubleday hardcover as:
Palau, Luis, 1934–
    Where is God when bad things happen?: finding solace in times of trouble / by Luis Palau with Steve Halliday. — 1st ed.
        p.   cm.
    Includes index.
    1. Suffering—Religious aspects—Christianity. 2. Consolation.
I. Halliday, Steve, 1957– . II. Title.
BV4909.P35   1999
248.8′6—dc21   98-40734
                                                          CIP

ISBN 0-385-49264-2

Copyright © 1999 by Luis Palau

All Rights Reserved
Printed in the United States of America
First Galilee Edition: June 2000

10 9 8 7 6 5 4 3 2

CONTENTS

Where
Is God
When Bad
Things Happen?

INTRODUCTION

LOOKING FOR HOPE

Last night I sat down in front of the television set and began to flip through the channels. A scene from some movie flashed on the screen, featuring a woman and her male companion as they sat waiting in a car.

"I've got only six months to live," she says.

"Well, I hope you believe in God," he replies.

"Believe in a God who's going to kill me before I'm twenty-five?" the young woman asks bitterly. "I don't think so."

While this young woman's character is fictional, her outlook certainly isn't. I've met her thousands of times while talking with individuals reeling from similar kinds of disasters. Today, more than at almost any other time in history, men and women are responding to personal tragedy by turning their backs on God and trying to walk through life on their own.

You've probably heard about William and Michael Randall, active members of a California Boy Scout troop who were kicked out of the organization when they refused to recite the part of the oath that acknowledges a Scout's duty to God.

Both twins are atheists. Their mother, Valerie, a former Methodist, considers herself an unbeliever, and their father, James, once planned to become a Baptist minister—until he served as a medical lab technician during the Vietnam War. There he saw such unspeakable atrocities that he gave up his pastoral dreams and concluded that we are all alone, adrift in a hostile universe.

"If there was a God, he wouldn't have allowed so many young boys to be blown up and killed," James told one reporter. "No God would allow that kind of suffering to go on."

And James is not unique. Millions of men and women around

the planet have been confronted with horrifying evil of one stripe or another and have decided—some reluctantly, others angrily—that either God does not exist or that He is impotent and therefore irrelevant. They cannot conceive how a loving, all-powerful God could witness such horrors and not seem to move a finger to prevent them. And they cry out,

Where was God when . . .

   . . . my baby was born severely deformed?
   . . . a student opened fire on others at school?
   . . . I was raped repeatedly as a twelve-year-old?
   . . . thousands died in last year's killer earthquake?
   . . . I lost my job for no good reason?
   . . . my spouse walked out on me for someone else?

I hear such cries all the time, and the anguish that fills each weeping syllable never ceases to move me deeply. For one thing, they remind me of my own personal agonies (more about that in Chapter 1). But second, those cries move me so profoundly because I believe there exists an unfailing salve for all wounds, a potent balm for all injuries—not a magic cure, but a final one. And I want all whom I meet to discover it for themselves.

To that end I host an occasional TV program called "Night Talk with Luis Palau" that has been broadcast live in dozens of major cities. We invite viewers to call in with their questions and troubles and try to point them in a proven direction toward healing and hope. Many of their stories are retold in this book.

Of course, I can speak with only a small fraction of those who phone us. Those who don't get through to me are helped by well-trained individuals who offer personal and informed assistance. But whether on the air or in private, we aim to handle every caller with compassion and understanding. No topic is out of bounds; we talk openly and honestly with everyone who takes the time to reach us.

Still, I have learned not to speak at length about purely theoretical questions. I used to spend a lot of time answering questions such as "What does God think of abortion?" But I don't do that anymore. I don't want to take valuable air time to answer hypothetical inquiries about a third party. I want to answer real-life questions from hurting people struggling right now with some painful issue. When I get hypothetical questions these days, I usually say something like "I'll tell you in a minute what God thinks about that, but I'm far more interested in knowing this: Are you talking about yourself or someone you know, or is this just a theoretical question?" If it's merely theoretical, I say, "I will answer your question because that's what I'm here for. But I want to help people actually going through personal troubles; I'm not that interested in answering brain teasers." And a minute later I move to the next caller.

Why do this? Because I'm much more concerned with helping people than I am in trying to provide a philosophical explanation for the problem of evil. I'm not a philosopher; I long to introduce people to the Great Physician, not to the *Complete Works of Plato*. I often ask people, "What brought you to Jesus Christ? Why did you listen to the Gospel in the first place?" In so many cases, it was a crisis: divorce, illness, unemployment, an accident, death.

I have written *Where Is God When Bad Things Happen?* to help individuals like yourself come to grips with the crushing adversities of life by pointing to the limitless resources found in God alone. Without sidestepping hard questions or slipping into the pat answers of a merely intellectual faith, I try to provide encouragement and hope to those who sorely need both.

BEFORE YOU BEGIN

I assume you picked up this book because you're honestly searching for answers to difficult questions prompted by a tragedy in your life. May I recommend that, even before you read my book, you take some time to read a few choice passages from the Bible. To get yourself ready for what I have to say, why not give yourself some spiritual reading from God's Word? I suggest you get your spirit in tune with what follows by reading and pondering the following Scriptures:

- Psalm 34
- Psalm 46
- Isaiah 43:1–13
- Matthew 7:7–14
- Romans 8

I have no reason to hide for a minute my profound belief that God can meet all of your needs. I know that multitudes of people who have seen or been touched personally by tragedy wonder if God cares—or even if He exists. I'll tackle these difficult questions head-on, yet let me say right up front that I will continually point back to God as the ultimate answer.

I cannot give a satisfying explanation for why some things happen, nor can I address everything that's on your mind. But I can do one thing: I can offer you a way to find hope, peace, and a future. I believe most people want to believe in God—not be angry with Him. In my experience, most people long for a settled mind. They want peace, forgiveness, and freedom from overpowering feelings of guilt. If that describes you, you've come to the right place.

Chapter 1 outlines some of my own personal challenges and questions about "Where Is God When Bad Things Happen?" while Chapters 2 through 12 tackle tragedies ranging from premature death to birth defects. Since every chapter in Part II is self-contained, I suggest you turn first to the chapter that addresses the problem most troublesome to you. For example, if you grew up in a dysfunctional home, I recommend you start with Chapter 4, "Home, Sour Home." If you struggle with serious health issues, I suggest you begin with Chapter 6, "I'm Afraid I Have Some Bad News for You . . ." Chapters 13 and 14 conclude the book by stepping back from individual tragedies to look at the larger picture.

While I believe that *Where Is God When Bad Things Happen?* should help all readers, it is meant especially for those without any current faith commitment who yet wonder where God is in times of acute personal trouble. This is not an academic treatise on "the problem of pain," nor is it a sterile theological meditation on human suffering. Instead, it is an empathetic, passionate exploration of divine action in the midst of terrible human pain. Therefore, it is a book for all those who cry out for some measure of solace, hope, and understanding when confronted by unexpected tragedy.

As I said, my goal is to draw you back to God. Won't you give God a chance to reveal Himself personally to you? God is not vengeful, and He does not inflict tragedy on us out of spite. I pray that *Where Is God When Bad Things Happen?* will be of great help to you.

PART ONE

1

FOUR STRIKES
DOESN'T MEAN YOU'RE OUT

When tragedy shatters the comfortable rhythms of life, most of us—after we lift our bleeding bodies from the floor—ask just one question: *Why?* Why did this happen? Why did this happen to *me?* If there really is a God, and if He is a God of love as most people of faith claim, then how could He have allowed such an awful tragedy into my life? What kind of a God could sit back and do nothing?

"Just where was God when this incident demolished my world?" we demand. This isn't merely an intellectual question for me.

First, I deal with individuals every day whose lives have been torn apart by tragedy. They don't want "academic" answers to their pain; they frantically search for any shred of real hope on which they might steady their trembling hands. They need to see a future hidden somewhere beneath the rubble of their lives.

Second, I know something about tragedy firsthand. At least four times in my life, family catastrophes seemed to fall like meteors out of the sky, obliterating my view of the future and nearly burying me alive beneath their fearsome weight. Each time my knees buckled and I was tempted to ask God, "Where *were* You when this happened?"

And so I write this book not from some insulated, theoretical viewpoint, but from an intensely personal perspective.

GOOD-BYE, DAD

The first "meteor" slammed into my life when I was ten years old, away at a British boarding school located north of Buenos Aires, Argentina. There I received a telephone call from my grandmother—a call that would change my life.

"Luis," she said nervously, "your father is very sick. You need to come home right away."

I loved my dad. He was a successful businessman who emigrated to Argentina from Spain when he was a boy, along with his parents and brothers and sisters. His father died a few years later, when my dad was about sixteen. He had to go to work very early in life. He bought a pickup truck and began to haul construction materials for builders—bricks, cement, sand, whatever they needed.

As his business grew, he began thinking, *I can build houses as well as these fellows. Why should I just haul their stuff?* Soon he bought some land and began a housing development. He didn't force his buyers to sign contracts; he counted on their goodwill to pay him. His business boomed, and he began to make good money. He brought his brothers into the business and began hiring other employees.

Dad bought a small farm and hired maids and nannies and drivers to make it work. Townspeople respected him, and I remember thinking, *My dad's big stuff.* He promised that when I turned sixteen he would buy me a pickup—a big deal in our little village. He also gave me a piece of land and helped me plant corn and tomatoes there. He said it was my piece of property.

My dad's soul prospered along with his business. He became a Christian at age twenty-six, shortly after my mom made her own commitment to Jesus Christ. In the middle of a Sunday service held at a tiny chapel, he stood up, interrupted the preacher, and announced his decision to follow Jesus. He showed his commitment by remodeling the church, constructing other church buildings in the region, giving away modest new homes to several poorer families, and proclaiming Christ's Good News to hundreds.

And then one day my dad got sick. He was helping some of his employees to unload a shipment of sand, sweating like mad. He caught a chill and soon contracted bronchial pneumonia. It was the end of World War II, and no penicillin was available. Doctors had no other way to treat the infection. Within nine days he grew quite weak.

That's when I got the call. I knew he must be very sick; my grandmother would speak with such urgency for no other reason.

Immediately I took the train to a little town outside Buenos Aires, then walked home under a blistering summer sun. I doubt I walked more than a few blocks, but when you're ten and your dad is passing away, a few blocks seem like miles. By midafternoon I arrived home to turmoil. Various relatives were wailing and crying out, "Why did God allow this man to die? What about the orphans?" Even our dog was howling. My dad had slipped into eternity a few hours earlier—at only thirty-four years of age.

We buried my father the day after he died. Embalming was not widely practiced at that time, and Argentina's hot summer demanded a quick burial. Family members tried to keep my sisters and me away from the cemetery, but I escaped through a window and ran up to one of my dad's young employees. "Let me go, too," I said, and jumped into the back of his truck, covering myself with a tarp.

I had vowed to throw the first clump of dirt on our dad's casket; as the oldest child, I felt I had the right. When we got to the cemetery, I jumped out of the truck and scooted between all the men standing by the graveside. Before any of them could stop me, I threw the first clod of earth on my dad's coffin.

Life changed drastically after that. It was now me, my three sisters, our mother, and a fourth sister born the following spring. Mom didn't know anything about running a business, and over the next few years the debts piled up. Many unscrupulous people cheated her, and we plummeted from wealth to utter poverty. I remember as a teenager wearing donated suits that were too long and overcoats massively out of proportion for my scrawny body. Eventually—mostly out of embarrassment—we moved to Córdoba, a few hundred miles north. We had been the wealthiest family in town, and now we were the poorest. In response to our most earnest prayers, God sometimes seemed silent.

Ultimately I had to forgo my graduate-school dreams and start working to help support my mom and four sisters. At one point we owed eight months' rent with no ability to pay; only through God's mercy did our landlord not throw us out on the street. The time came when all we had to eat for dinner was a loaf of French bread seasoned with garlic. The owner of a corner shop gave us the loaves because he knew we had nothing else. Today I look at pictures taken of me in those days and find it hard to believe I was ever so thin.

More than once when we were truly down, at the brink of collapse and without the smallest coin to our name, we would receive a letter. "Mrs. Palau," it might say, "you probably don't know me, and if we were to meet, you wouldn't remember me. But when you were liquidating your property after your husband's death, I cheated you. I said that the truck I bought from you was no good, that the motor was cracked and useless, but that as a mercy I would take it off your hands and use it for parts. In fact, it was in perfect order. I've been unable to live with myself all these years. I'm enclosing a check for the true value of the truck, plus interest."

Sometimes we received word that funds had been sent and were available in town for collection. Short even of bus fare, my mother walked several miles to retrieve the check. These occasional blessings allowed us to buy food and other necessities—and we kids took note.

BATTLING CANCER

A second meteor blazed into my night sky years later in 1980 when my wife, Pat, and I faced the biggest challenge of our lives together.

Pat had joined me for the last six weeks of ministry in Glasgow, Scotland. Her unusual quiet, coupled with her long face, let me know something was up. One day I finally asked what troubled her. She said she hadn't wanted to tell me for fear that the news would distract from the work at hand. And then she named the problem.

"I've got a lump in my breast," she said, "and I fear that it's bad."

Greatly alarmed, we returned home to the States and made a Monday-morning appointment to see the doctor. A biopsy was taken, and we were instructed to return on Thursday. We prayed and hoped for the best.

On Thursday we heard the words no one wants to hear. "I'm really sorry, but this is a malignant tumor," the doctor told us. "Pat, you need to come to the hospital this Sunday; surgery is scheduled for Monday. There can be no delay. We don't know how far it has spread, but you have cancer."

As we walked out of the doctor's office, stunned and in shock, Pat turned to me and said, "Well, babe, this is the end."

Pat underwent a modified radical mastectomy, and the doctors prescribed a longer-than-usual regimen of chemotherapy. The treatments gave her such nausea that she told me, "I'd rather die than go through this." After two weeks the doctors lowered her dose of chemo. Even this seemed to freeze her body. She shivered constantly; heating pads and electric blankets provided no relief. It was awful for two long years.

POLIO FROM A CUBE

It's not always a great honor to be singled out as "one of only four people who . . ." It certainly wasn't in my mother-in-law's case. This saintly woman was one of only four people who, thirty-five years ago, received a tainted dose of Dr. Jonas Salk's polio-vaccine cube and subsequently came down with the crippling disease.

Pat and I were speaking at a conference when we received word that Elsie Scofield, Pat's mother, had been rushed to a hospital and could be dying. At age forty-eight she took one of the cubes as a precautionary measure and within days found herself fighting for life. From that day her legs have been paralyzed.

The incident profoundly shook us up. It didn't make any sense. First, she really didn't need to take the vaccine. Second, she had a five-year-old son at home who needed a healthy mom. And third, Elsie was a godly woman who certainly didn't "deserve" what she received.

AIDS TOUCHES THE FAMILY

In recent years one of my sisters and her husband have served on staff with a very large church in California. Before that, they lived in beautiful Buenos Aires, Argentina. One of their sons, Kenneth, was a brilliant, charming, good-looking young man gifted with such musical talent that he earned a spot with the Buenos Aires symphony. Early in his teenage years, however, he began to show signs of rebellion.

By the time his family moved to the San Francisco Bay area, Kenneth had adopted a homosexual lifestyle and began to visit the big city to see his many "boyfriends." He never tried to hide his behavior from anyone; he was a cocksure young man who thought he could beat the world. He'd even bring his lovers to his parents' home, despite their firm rejection of his sexual behavior.

One day Kenneth started feeling ill and made an appointment for an exam at the Stanford University Medical Center in Palo Alto. After many tests, his doctor told him solemnly, "Kenneth, I'm sorry to tell you that you have AIDS. You have six months to live. It's full-blown, and there's nothing I can do."

From that point on we all watched and prayed as my twenty-three-year-old nephew withered away. He lost weight and grew progressively weaker. He hung on for two years, outlasting his doctor's prediction by a year and half. Only in the last few weeks of his life did he grow too weak to indulge his passion for singing. Finally, about five years ago, his multiplying sores and cancers grew too much for his decimated body, and he died at age twenty-five.

WHERE WAS GOD?

Each time one of these meteors rocked my world, the "Where was God?" question raised plenty of dust—and at first I lacked a good answer for it. All I had was my firm trust in the goodness and faithfulness of Almighty God, even when I couldn't give clear answers as to His whereabouts. God owes us no answers, of course.

Still, over the years, as I've pondered this question, I have come to see that—in most cases, anyway—it really does have an answer.

Today, for example, I can give the following answers to the questions that troubled me.

I believe that my father's death kept me from simply heading off to college and into the business world and instead set me on the track I've now followed for many years. There are certainly a lot of good reasons for becoming a businessman, of course, but God had something different for me.

I am convinced that if it hadn't been for my dad's early death, I probably wouldn't be involved in full-time ministry to others. My dad died with such hope that I thought everybody should die that way. I want everybody to know Jesus Christ. The beloved apostle John tells us in the Bible that "God has given us [who believe] eternal life, and this life is in his Son" (1 John 5:11). Belief in Jesus is the only way to die sure of heaven.

I believe Christian suffering can be part of God's redemptive purpose in some unusual way. That is, God can take our pain and use it for amazing purposes; He does not waste our tears. The Bible hints at this when the apostle Paul says, "I fill up in my flesh what is still lacking in regard to Christ's afflictions" (Colossians 1:24).

Pat's battle with cancer demonstrates this principle. She was in chemo and didn't return with me to Scotland for an evangelistic campaign, so everyone wanted to know how she was doing. The British Broadcasting Corporation in Scotland asked me to close off the day's broadcasting with a seven-minute program. For eight nights in a row I described my wife's cancer and told a huge listening audience how she had found hope in Jesus Christ.

The BBC also challenged me to walk into a Glasgow pub and talk with patrons about the Lord—they didn't think I had the guts. So I said, "Sure I will." I told them what pub I'd visit and they said they'd be there. The next morning I walked into the pub and began talking to the guys. Most of them knew who I was from all the media exposure, and many were cowering in dark corners, not knowing what to do.

When the BBC guys finally showed up, the patrons started disappearing. Nobody wanted to be seen in a pub at 11 A.M. on a working day. When the BBC crew started filming, I was talking to a young man. We had a good conversation.

That night when I arrived at the Kelvin Hall in Glasgow, a young woman volunteering as a Christian counselor came running up to me and exclaimed, "Oh, Mr. Palau, you won't believe what happened. I've been the only Christian in my family for years. My father's been an alcoholic; he drinks whiskey like it's water, just cases and cases of it. My mom is a non-Christian; my brother is out of work. This morning you went to a pub and one of the young men you talked with just happened to be my brother! He came running home after that and said, 'You won't believe who was at the pub! Mr. Palau was at the pub!' It made quite an impression on him."

But her story didn't stop there. That same day her father was sitting in front of the television, more than half drunk, watching me describe my wife's battle with cancer. He began mocking me, sure I was just another phony American evangelist. But the story touched his heart, and finally he collapsed in tears. Somehow it got through to the old Scotsman. At the end of the short program, I said, "If you're watching and you haven't received Jesus Christ, get on your knees by the TV set and open your heart to him." And this old man did just that! Then he called his family and said, "I've been converted! I'm a Christian!" He asked them all to come to the house, led them to a cabinet where he kept his whiskey, and invited them to watch as he poured it all down the toilet.

When this young lady told me her story, I thought, *Could it be that the Lord, in some mysterious way, allowed Pat's suffering in order to bring this old drunk to Jesus Christ? Maybe her suffering was meant to be redemptive after all.*

I believe that's one angle. There may be other purposes, other reasons I don't know and probably couldn't fully understand this side of eternity. But I do know that Pat's story may have been the only thing that could have converted that hard old man.

Why did my mother-in-law take one of the world's only four tainted polio cubes and have to suffer half her life with paralysis? To be honest, I don't know. I can see how her gracious and generous spirit and her refusal to live in bitterness have deeply affected those she knows. She's a living witness to the power of God.

But why did God not use that power to keep my wife's mother from getting polio in the first place? No one really knows. But her case reminds me that if we're not able to look beyond all the suffering to the controlling, overruling hand of God, we're really on our own. And I've seen too much of God's good hand to believe that's true.

My nephew's story proves that the Lord is gracious and will forgive, even at the last moment.

Kenneth told his extended family about his AIDS diagnosis at a family reunion in the hills of Northern California. Sixty of us had gathered to celebrate my mom's seventy-fifth birthday, and he took the occasion to announce that he had been living a homosexual lifestyle, had contracted the HIV virus, and had been given a death sentence. It shocked the whole family.

Kenneth's parents and I knew his story before his announcement, but at that point my sister turned to me and said, "You've got to find out if he's really repented or not. He claims he has, but we don't believe him." So I went for a walk with my nephew up in the hills, just the two of us. "Kenneth," I asked him, "do you have eternal life? Have you truly repented? You just told the whole family you're going to die. Are you going to heaven?"

"Uncle Luis," he replied, "I repented and I believe I have eternal life and I'm going to heaven—but my dad doesn't believe me. He thinks I'm just putting on an act because I know the Bible well. He won't believe that I truly have repented. When I die, will you convince him that I have repented and that God has forgiven me and that I know I'm going to heaven?"

I came away from that conversation convinced that my nephew truly was a changed person. And in the few months he had left, he was able to demonstrate his conversion to his whole family. He often talked about the Lord, and family members regularly read the Bible to him. He also kept his humor to the end. My mom was growing old and my sister had bought a family burial plot. It was decided that whoever died first, Kenneth or my mother, would be buried beneath the other. So Kenneth would say, "Grandma, whether I die first or you, from time to time I'll tap on your casket to see how you're doing."

Kenneth's body is on the bottom. But he doesn't do any tapping. Both he and my mom are far too busy enjoying eternity with the Lord in heaven.

LOOKING FOR ANSWERS

As we look into the lives of other individuals who have cried out in agony, "Where was God when . . . ?" we will return again and again in this book to the conviction that He was there all along. Sometimes He's in the shadows. Sometimes He's underneath us, holding us in His arms. But always He's right there, even if we can't see Him.

The fact is, no matter what tragedies befall us, we *can* find hope—if we keep looking in the right places.

PART
TWO

BUT SHE'S TOO
YOUNG TO DIE!

What do you tell a devastated young couple who awakens one morning to find their infant daughter lying cold and still beside them—a victim of sudden infant death syndrome? That was my challenge one night in Kansas City.

Greg and his wife, Linda, had waited for two days to get on "Night Talk with Luis Palau," and his trembling voice told me his heart was breaking.

"I lost my daughter Gabriella a week ago," he said. "She was ten weeks old; I lost her to SIDS. And I'm just wondering—why?"

On its own that's a difficult question to answer. But Greg wasn't finished yet.

"You know, as a father you're supposed to protect and provide for your children, and I feel as if I've failed. Luis, she lay right in between us in our bed, and that's where she died! I mean, she was not but six inches away from us. There must have been something I could have done. I just wanted to end my life and go see her, because I loved her very much!

"I'm thirty-two years old, I've waited and waited to have a child of my own, and I've always wanted a little girl. God gave me what I wanted—and then He took it away just as quickly as He gave it."

My heart ached for this man as I pondered what could be said. How could I bring some hope and comfort to his shattered soul? I'll tell you what I said to Greg and Linda that night, but before I do, permit me to take you thousands of miles from their deep sorrow and introduce you to a man who also bitterly grieved the loss of his own sweetheart daughter.

Picture this scene: an English graveyard in Bristol, deserted except for a solitary, despairing man. It is Saturday, and the man has come to this lonely place—as he has for six months of Saturdays—to speak his anguish to a mute headstone.

"Alice," he says softly, "we miss you terribly. We love you so very much. We had such dreams for you, such hopes. And now they are all gone. Oh, how we miss you!"

Alice, the man's delicate ten-and-a-half-year-old daughter, had died in November after a short illness. The following June this distraught man attended a business luncheon at which I was the speaker. He happened to sit across the table from a friend of mine and heard a message typical of those I offer to an audience of professionals. During part of the talk the man began to sob.

After the luncheon my friend said to him, "You look really distressed. Is there something I can do?"

"I have gone through an unspeakable tragedy," he replied.

"So have I," our friend said. "My husband left me abruptly; I had no notion it was about to happen."

"Mine was my little daughter, Alice, a beautiful girl," he said. "She contracted an incurable disease and the doctors could do nothing. We buried her last November, and I can't get over it. I am devastated. My wife is still in a state of shock. We just don't know how God relates to all this. Our little girl loved the Lord with all her heart. Now she's gone." The man seemed totally helpless and miserable—no church, no personal knowledge of God, a practical agnostic.

Our friend consoled the man and then invited him to one of our stadium meetings. His deep distress prevented him from catching much of what I had said at the luncheon, but he agreed to return that night. After the evening meeting we held a little reception, to which our friend brought this man and his wife. I met them and listened to their gut-wrenching story. Then I told them I planned to preach on heaven the following night.

"Why don't you come and hear the message on heaven?" I asked. "Maybe that will clarify things for you."

The next morning he brought his surviving child, a nine-year-old boy, to our children's rally. He and his wife returned that night for the message on heaven, and at another reception one night later, a Saturday evening, he bore a message of his own.

"When we buried Alice, I wrote her a letter expressing how I felt about her and her life, about how much I was going to miss her and how bad we feel," he began. "I was in utter despair. I simply placed the letter on her chest when we closed the casket.

"Every Saturday morning since then, before heading to the golf course, I have visited the cemetery to stand in front of Alice's grave and to talk to my daughter about how deeply we all miss her."

His face betrayed terrible pain, but it betrayed something else, too—a deep peace seemed etched on his weary features.

"Last night when you were preaching on heaven, I gave my heart to Christ," he said. "And, you know, already I can see a change taking place in my life. This morning, when I got to the cemetery and stood by Alice's grave, it suddenly dawned on me: *Wait! Alice isn't here. She's in heaven. And now I'm going to go to heaven, too. I don't need to have an imaginary conversation with her!*

"I finally decided, right then and there, that I wasn't going to visit the grave every Saturday. Maybe I would come from time to time out of memory and respect, but I no longer have a compulsion as I did for all these months since she died. You see, it finally registered: *She isn't here.*"

So that morning he said, "Good-bye, Alice." And he left.

His story explained a parcel I received that night just before the service began. This dear father had sent to the platform a photograph of Alice with a little note attached: "Luis, please keep this picture of Alice with you so you can think of her."

At the reception I referred to his note and said to him, "Not only am I going to think about her, I'm going to talk about her all over the world. And I'm going to carry this picture with me."

To this day Alice's smiling face accompanies me on all of my travels.

WHAT DOES THE BIBLE SAY?

Both of these stories prompt the question "Where was God when my child died?" What can we say to those who have suddenly lost their dear little ones? Their deaths seem so wrong, so unfair. As one man, Nicholas Woltersdorff, wrote after losing his son in a climbing accident: "It's so wrong, so profoundly wrong, for a child to die before his parents. It's hard to bury our parents, but that we expect. Our parents belong to our past; our children belong to our future. We do not visualize our future without them. How can I bury my son, my future, my next in line? He was meant to bury me!"

I think there are at least seven things to say to someone in this kind of pain.

1. God sees our heartache and takes seriously our loss.

Our heavenly Father is not unmoved by our agony. He is not callused or distant. For good reason the Bible calls Him "the God of all comfort" (1 Corinthians 1:3).

It was Jesus who wept loudly when His friend Lazarus died—so loudly that witnesses said, "See how he loved him!" (John 11:36). When He saw a great calamity descending on Jerusalem, it was also Jesus who cried out, "How often I have longed to gather your children together, as a hen gathers her children under her wings!" (Matthew 23:37). Centuries before this, it was God the Father who proclaimed through the prophet Isaiah, "Comfort, comfort my people, says your God. Speak tenderly to Jerusalem" (Isaiah 40:1).

If you have suffered the loss of a little one, know that God longs to comfort your broken heart. He is very near to you right now, and He wants to restore your wounded soul.

2. Every life is a complete life, even though it may not look that way to us.

The Bible says, "All the days ordained for me were written in your book before one of them came to be" (Psalm 139:16). That means God knows exactly how long each of us will live. Some miscarry; some live more than a century. But every life is a complete life. We may not understand this completely—and accepting it will never take all the sting out of our loss—but embracing this as truth can help to soften the blow. Whether a life spans decades or blooms and fades in minutes, it is a complete life. God makes no mistakes.

3. God loves little children and will welcome them all into heaven.

I believe that children like Alice and Gabriella are in heaven with Jesus right now. Jesus loved little children and even used them as examples of how we adults might come into a right relationship with God. "Let the little children come to me, and do not hinder them, for the kingdom of heaven belongs to such as these" (Matthew 19:14), Jesus declared to His astonished disciples.

Hints of this special concern for infants and young children are given even in the Old Testament. For example, when King David lost his baby boy to an illness, he said to the members of his court, "I will go to him, but he will not return to me" (2 Samuel 12:23). I don't think he was merely saying he would one day die, as his son had. I believe he was proclaiming his firm belief that he would see his son in heaven.

It is inconceivable to me that a gracious, loving God would ever condemn a child to hell. I believe that the work of Jesus Christ covers such children and that they all will greet us in heaven.

That is why I could say to Greg, who desperately wanted to hold his daughter again, "I believe the Bible teaches that your little girl is in heaven in the presence of the Lord, and that you will see her one day if you have Jesus Christ in your life as your Savior and Master. I believe that she is saved through the work of Jesus Christ, that she is redeemed and rescued by the grace and goodness of God. *Greg, you will see your girl in heaven.* She is enjoying life, she's rejoicing. And I'll tell you, Greg—she is contented there in the presence of God. Your little Gabriella is in the arms of the Lord—thoroughly conscious, perfect, and forever in the presence of Jesus Christ."

4. God has purposes that we cannot understand.

We can never understand all the ways of God. We who have a difficult time programming our VCRs and figuring out how to put together certain children's toys should not be surprised that the One who created the universe and keeps it running also thinks and acts in ways we can't begin to fathom.

"My thoughts are not your thoughts, neither are my ways your ways," the Lord reminds us. "As the heavens are higher than the earth, so are my ways higher than your ways and my thoughts than your thoughts" (Isaiah 55:8–9). We are not always kept in the dark, yet some things are beyond our understanding: "The secret things belong to the LORD our God, but the things revealed belong to us and to our children forever" (Deuteronomy 29:29).

As I told Greg, "God has a purpose for each one of us, even for little Gabriella's ten weeks. Of course, we don't always understand the ways of God; He has mysteries we can't comprehend. Why would He take a little girl? I don't know—but God makes no mistakes. Sometimes we foolishly think He does, but He doesn't. He had a plan for your little girl, and it was somehow fulfilled."

I admit it's terribly hard to understand why God would take a little one whom we love so much and for whom we held such big dreams. Right now, at this moment, none of us can fully understand why. But I'm convinced that in heaven we *will* understand. When the apostle Paul writes, "Now we see but a poor reflection as in a mirror; then we shall see face to face. Now I know in part; then I shall know fully, even as I am fully known" (1 Corinthians 13:12–13), I think he was telling us that all these earthly mysteries that so puzzle and hurt us will one day be solved. The darkness surrounding our tragedies will be dispelled by blazing, divine light. And then we will see and appreciate the stunning grandeur and majesty of God's total plan. But that day is not yet.

5. God may be protecting them from something far worse later in life.
I know not everyone believes this, but I do. God sees the end from the beginning, and it may be that He takes home certain loved ones now because He knows that later on a tragedy of much grimmer proportions would overtake them. No doubt someone will say to me, "But if God is almighty, couldn't He prevent either tragedy from happening in the first place?" Yes, He could—but that's not the way this world works. Which brings us to the next point.

6. We are part of a fallen human race.

This world is not as it should be. God created it perfect in the beginning, but something happened to shatter its original harmony and beauty and peace. The Bible says that when our first forebears, Adam and Eve, chose to disobey God and rebel against His rule, a curse settled on the human race and on the world and universe we inhabit. Their sin brought to the human race all the ugliness and corruption and hatred and depravity and brutality and illness and death that we see everywhere around us today.

This means that death is an unwanted part of this current world order. As the great Oxford writer C. S. Lewis once said, "Wars don't cause death. Wars simply hurry the process for some people." All of us will die; it's just a question of when.

The sad fact is that until God remakes this world and lifts the curse—and He will do so one glorious day!—horrible things will continue to happen on this planet "that just isn't right." In this world gone awry, the good do not always receive their just due, nor do the evil. Jesus said that God "causes his sun to rise on the evil and the good, and sends rain on the righteous and the unrighteous" (Matthew 5:45)—and sometimes that sun causes firestorms that incinerate both the evil and the good, and those rains create floods that drown both the righteous and the unrighteous.

7. The people closest to God have never been immune to painful circumstances.

It certainly does not seem fair to most of us that innocent children in the bloom of life can die from awful diseases or accidents, while many evil adults live for eight or nine decades in the lap of luxury. It just doesn't seem right.

But I can never forget that the most unfair death of all was that of Jesus Christ. Although God repeatedly called Jesus His "beloved Son" (Matthew 3:17; 12:18; 17:5), His life was taken that we might gain eternal life. The apostle Peter put it like this: "For Christ died for sins once for all, the righteous for the unrighteous, to bring you to God" (1 Peter 3:18).

Paul the apostle said the same thing in these words: "God made him who had no sin [Jesus] to be sin for us, so that in him [Jesus] we might become the righteousness of God" (2 Corinthians 5:21).

**Walnut Hill
Church Library
Bethel, CT 06801**

Jesus' death was not "fair" in any usual sense of the term, yet He freely gave His life for us so that we might become sons and daughters of God. It is His most "unfair" death that gives us the firm hope that we will one day see again all our precious loved ones who left this earth at such a tender age. "Let the little children come to me," Jesus said—and then He died on a cross to make it possible.

WHAT TO DO NOW

I hope the answers I've just suggested give some clarity and bring some hope to those of you who have suffered the devastating loss of a child. I don't want to leave you with answers only, however. Allow me briefly to sketch out a few practical steps you might consider taking to help yourself recover from such a stunning blow.

First, there are a number of things you can do on your own to find healing from your wounds.

• *Spend time with God.*

Say to Him, "Lord, what lessons am I to learn from thi. traumatic experience? What do You want me to do now? How ca we redeem any part of this experience?"

Books like this one can be helpful up to a point, but the real answers to the difficult questions of life are best found right at the source: God Himself. Middlemen have their place, but that's all they are—individuals in the middle. Some of their advice is useful, some isn't. What you need most is to talk to the One who can really give you insight into your sorrow and medicine for your soul.

In the nicest way possible, I have to say, "Don't ask me, go ask God yourself." That is where the answers can be found.

• *Think a lot about heaven.*

I heard recently that young people are more interested in death than in almost any other subject. That can be frightening, but it can also be used for good. Thinking and studying about heaven are not an exercise in wishful thinking, but a fruitful and encouraging endeavor that enables us to live well now.

Walnut Hill
Church Library
Bethel, CT 06801

But you have to go to the right source for your information about heaven. Boatloads of nonsense are circulating these days on the subject. The only trustworthy information we have about the hereafter is found in God's Word, the Bible, not in bestselling books by people who claim to have visited there or channeled there or flown there first class on a flying saucer.

And what we find in the Bible is that heaven is a real place. Even children understand that (sometimes better than we adults). A friend of mine told me of an incident involving a seven-year-old boy named Peter. The boy heard his parents talking at the breakfast table one morning about a family friend, Mr. Whittle. Word had come that Mr. Whittle was close to death and about to go to heaven. When Peter heard this, he got up and ran to his bedroom. My friend thought the boy was shaken up and so left him alone. When Peter returned to the table, he said, "Dad, would you send this to Mr. Whittle?" The note said, "Dear Mr. Whittle, I hear that you're going to heaven. Isn't that great? Love, Peter." Even though death is an enemy, going to heaven truly is great.

When thinking of heaven, many people ask, "Do our loved ones go directly to heaven, or do they go to some in-between place?" According to the Bible, on their death believers go directly to be with Jesus. As the apostle Paul put it, "to be away from the body" is to be "at home with the Lord" (2 Corinthians 5:8). Knowing this certainty can do much to ease the transition from earth to heaven when that day finally comes.

Many years ago the founder of a well-respected Christian college on the West Coast, Dr. Willard Aldrich, was sitting with his mother. She was in her nineties and could hardly eat anymore. Every noon he visited her house to feed her a cup of soup or to give her a little rice. Mrs. Aldrich had been a fine believer and follower of Jesus Christ all her life, and she knew the end was coming. One day Dr. Aldrich walked into her room bringing soup and a few little biscuits. He sat by his mother and noticed her all dressed up with her hair fixed nicely, and he asked, "Mother, why are you all dressed up today?" She replied, "Willard, I'm going home today, that's why." He thought she was disoriented, so he said to her, "Mother, you *are* home. What do you mean, you're going home?"

"Willard, I'm going to heaven today," she responded.

"Okay, Mother, that's wonderful," Dr. Aldrich said, "but why don't you have a little soup?"

"No, Willard, I'll have some when I get there."

"Okay," her son replied, "why don't you have some for the road, then?"

That night Mrs. Aldrich went to be with the Lord. And in heaven one day her son will see her again.

• *Prepare your other children to understand death.*

If you have other children in the family, learn to speak about heaven in proper terms. Describe heaven in the vivid language of the Bible.

Jesus promised us, "In my Father's house are many rooms; if it were not so, I would have told you. I am going there to prepare a place for you" (John 14:2).

The apostle Paul tells us, "For the Lord himself will come down from heaven, with a loud command, with the voice of the archangel, and with the trumpet call of God, and the dead in Christ will rise first. After that, we who are still alive and are left will be caught up together with them in the clouds to meet the Lord in the air. And so we will be with the Lord forever" (1 Thessalonians 4:16–17).

During one of our live "Night Talk" programs, I received a call from Laurie. Her ten-year-old son, Joshua, had contracted leukemia; just prior to her call the disease had relapsed after a bone-marrow transplant. "It doesn't look good," she told me through tears, adding that Joshua had just lost a friend who suffered from the same disease. "I'm having a hard time dealing with children getting this, and I'm trying to understand why God allows this to happen to children. Why does He put them through all this?" she asked.

After bringing what comfort I could, I told Laurie some of the things I've outlined in this chapter. During our conversation I learned that she already was teaching Joshua about the Bible's picture of heaven.

"I think you're doing the right thing in training your boy for heaven," I told this frightened thirty-one-year-old mother of two. "Help him to understand that heaven is his home, that he will see the Lord Jesus, that he will see thousands of believers. The Bible says that in heaven there will be no more crying, no more pain, no more tears. That world is not like this one. The Bible says there will be rejoicing and singing.

"And let this be a beautiful lesson for your younger son. Let people see that your trust in the Lord is not shaken and that you will not deny Him. Don't follow the path of millions of people who, when something goes wrong, immediately start blaspheming God and denying Him. The Lord must have a purpose in your experience, perhaps to share with others. So don't despair and don't let this divert you from trusting Him and continuing to rely on Him. The Lord could heal Joshua, but if He chooses not to do so, remember that He has a better purpose than you and I can see."

Beyond the things you can do on your own, there are other things you can do with people outside your own family. I urge you not to remove yourself from people or to hide inside your house. Don't become a hermit. As painful as your loss is, it won't help to disappear inside the four walls of your castle. Let me suggest some possible ways to reach out:

• *For the rest of your life, you will be uniquely qualified to show love and compassion to hurting, lonely children.*

Since you've suffered so much over the loss of your child, how about dedicating a good percentage of your time to helping children who are suffering and alone? After you have spent enough time recovering from your loss—and I realize this may take a while—why not consider a Big Brother or Big Sister program or something similar that reaches out to boys and girls who lack a set of parents? Of course, this child can never "substitute" for your own child, but he or she has real needs you can meet.

• *You will be especially equipped to comfort those who have lost children.*

Redeem your sorrow and give redemptive meaning to the pain of losing your child. God wants to use you to comfort other people who are going through their own shattering pain. The Bible says God "comforts us in all our troubles, so that we can comfort those in any trouble with the comfort we ourselves have received from God" (2 Corinthians 1:4). No one knows what it is like to lose a child except someone else who also has lost a child. Why not use your own painful experience to help another to walk a similar path? I think you will find that in giving, you will receive far more in return.

HOW DO YOU KNOW?

The same night that I took the call from Greg and Linda, I received another from Karen, a thirty-six-year-old in a high-risk pregnancy confined to partial bed rest. Ten months prior to her call, she and her husband had suffered their own tragedy. After struggling with infertility for several years, they finally had a set of triplets. But all three children died.

"After that happened," Karen said, "I went through some real depression and hard times. I had a lot of people who gave me a lot of clichés about 'This was God's will' and 'It happened for a reason.' But I just lost a lot of faith. I said, 'Don't even talk to me about God.'

"But eventually I started going to a Bible-study group because I was trying to figure it out, trying to find some answers. A lot of people have asked me, 'Have you been saved? Have you given your life to Christ?' To be honest, I don't even know what that means. I'm Methodist, my husband is Catholic. When people ask me that, I don't really know how to answer them.

"If I died tomorrow, what would happen to me? I don't know. I never have gone to an altar and thrown myself down and cried. So what does that mean? Does it mean that I've just gone through the motions my whole life? Aren't we all going to heaven? I just don't understand. It's like I'm stuck somewhere."

I was glad to explain to Karen the difference between being religious and having a personal relationship with the Lord Jesus Christ. I told her about a woman in Chicago who opened her heart to Christ after attending church for forty-two years. This woman told me, "You know, after forty-two years, finally, it happened! I opened my heart to Christ, and now I know that I have eternal life!"

"But *how* do you know?" Karen asked urgently. I then quoted a few of my favorite Bible verses, the first one from the Gospel of John: "To all who received him, to those who believed in his name, he gave the right to become children of God" (John 1:12). I gave her Jesus' personal promise: "I give them eternal life, and they shall never perish; no one can snatch them out of my hand" (John 10:28). And I also quoted a famous verse from the New Testament book of Romans: "Everyone who calls on the name of the Lord will be saved" (Romans 10:13). I then described how the Holy Spirit comes into a believer's life and confirms in his or her soul the reality of Jesus' presence.

Karen "got it," and I hope you do, too! You know, the assurance of eternal life is one of the great gifts of God. If you don't have that assurance, at this very moment Jesus Christ says to you, "I have made you and I know you. I have loved you and I gave my life for you. I am alive and I am calling you. If you give me your heart right now, I will forgive all your sins. I'll give you the Holy Spirit. And I'll give you eternal life and heaven as an ultimate blessing."

To meet Jesus Christ and to know Him is better than falling in love, better than anything in the world. He is the Creator, and He loves you. He wants to come into your life and to take despair and turn it into hope.

The old song is still right. "Jesus loves the little children, all the children of the world." We don't know why He sometimes chooses to bring them home to heaven before we're ready to see them go, but we can know that He loves them with a passion we simply can't explain. And when we put our trust in Him as our Savior, we can also know that we will see those precious children again. And what a day that will be!

"But, Luis, how can I have that assurance?" you may be asking.

Let me share the same Scripture verses that someone once shared with me. And allow me to personalize these verses, as my friend did for me: "If you, ——— [insert your name], confess with your mouth, 'Jesus is Lord,' and believe in your heart that God raised him from the dead, you, ———, will be saved. For it is with your heart that you, ————, believe and are justified, and it is with your mouth that you, ————, confess and are saved" (Romans 10:9–10).

Have you asked the Lord Jesus to save you—to forgive your sins, cleanse your heart, adopt you into God's family, and give you the sure hope of heaven? If not, why not stop right now, where you are, and in the quietness of your heart talk to God. You can place your trust in Him this very minute. The choice is yours.

You can talk to God using any words you wish, of course. I suggest that you pray the following prayer of commitment:

"Lord, I come before You humbly, in the midst of my heartache and sorrow. Yes, please forgive my sins. Thank You that Jesus died on the cross to cleanse my heart and rose again to give me new eternal life. Thank You that now I can enjoy the sure hope of heaven. Please keep my precious little one in Your dear care. I love You and will live for You all the days of my life. Amen."

If that's your prayer, congratulations!

Welcome to the family of God![1]

[1] If you've just committed your life to Jesus Christ, please write to me. I'll be glad to correspond with you and send you a free copy of my book, *Your New Life with Christ.* It's yours free for the asking. Or maybe you would like to request prayer. Again, please feel free to write. My address is Luis Palau, P.O. Box 1173, Portland, Oregon 97207, U.S.A. E-mail: palau@palau.org.

WHEN YOUR
PERFECT BABY ISN'T

Sometimes life can seem even crueler than death. Why is it that some babies are born with severe mental or physical impairments? When young parents are confronted with the news that they must rear a child who will never be able to function at an intellectual level of more than a six-month-old, how can they fit a loving God into the equation? Where was God when their baby was forming in the womb?

In my experience, those who reject God almost always refer to suffering children as the one overwhelming reason they do so. "If there were a God, he wouldn't allow something like this to happen," they say. "I can't believe in a God who would permit such horrible things."

I can understand why they feel that way. The suffering of children seems so senseless, so cruel, so inexplicable. It raises one of the most difficult questions to answer. And yet I don't think it disproves the existence of a loving, omnipotent God, nor do I think it makes faith in Him either impossible or distasteful. In fact, in talking to families who live with severely disabled children, I have found that it's precisely a strong faith in a loving, omnipotent God that gives them hope and a reason for living.

AN ACCURATE PREDICTION

The night Fred Bass graduated from high school, his father took him aside and said, "Fred, life has been fun for you so far. It's going to get tougher from now on." Fred had no idea how accurate his father's prediction would turn out to be.

Fred and his wife Wendy became first-time parents on January 18, 1978, with the birth of their daughter Jaime. From the beginning, Jaime seemed "floppy" to her mother—she couldn't roll over and raise her head like most other kids. Friends and family and even the family doctor told Wendy not to worry, that all children develop at different speeds.

But when Jaime suffered her first seizure at six months, her parents took her to a specialist, who immediately identified several serious physical problems. Still, no one could label the cause of Jaime's disorder, and the Bass family held out hope that "in time she'll get better. She'll catch up." At two years of age Jaime was still very pretty, although she couldn't talk, walk, or stand. It was then that another specialist took Fred and Wendy aside and said, "This isn't fixable. Jaime is not going to get better." He painted what at the time seemed like a bleak picture; the reality, it turned out, would be far worse.

Jaime suffered from severe mental retardation, never advancing mentally beyond six to twelve months. Her muscles never developed properly, and she was unable to walk or control her spastic movements. She never learned to speak, had to be diapered until her death, constantly drooled, and was legally blind. She also suffered from an uncontrolled seizure disorder.

Fred and Wendy spent forty thousand dollars on tests to learn what caused these handicaps, but still doctors could tell them nothing. Jaime's condition was one in a million, they said. Trusting their words, the Basses had a second child, Aaron, who was born healthy and normal in 1981. Encouraged, Fred and Wendy decided to have a third child.

Joel was born April 11, 1985, and right away Wendy noticed "something wasn't right." In his first month she took her youngest son to the doctor, who told her not to worry—it was nearly impossible Joel could suffer from Jaime's unidentified disease. "Bring Joel back at three months for a thorough checkup," he instructed. After that next appointment the doctor, with ashen face, announced, "I'm so sorry. You were right; I should have listened to you. Joel apparently has the same problem as Jaime."

Jaime's symptoms had been only gradually diagnosed, "but with Joel it was like a bucket of cold water," Wendy says. "I asked God, 'What are you doing here? Wasn't one enough? What haven't I learned?' "

But life went on. Jaime seemed to get a tiny bit better every year until she reached age sixteen; she even managed to walk a little with the help of a walker. But that year Fred and Wendy realized with shock that their daughter's "rare metabolic degenerative disease" would in fact kill her, and probably soon. "She really started going downhill," Wendy said, "and I thought, *You mean I'm going to have to sit here and watch her die? I just can't!*"

At that point Fred and Wendy began to worry about what might happen to Jaime and Joel if their parents were taken out of the picture. Medical experts said that if they didn't place the two children in a care facility by the time they were eighteen, it would never happen. So a month before Jaime turned seventeen, she entered a foster-care home. Fred and Wendy struggled with the decision for a long time. Logically, placing Jaime in the home was the right thing to do; emotionally, it was not. They brought her home on weekends and for special occasions, and she cried every time she returned to the foster home.

Why, God? Wendy pleaded. *Why are You doing this? She should be home with family. Why do we have to do this?* It was the start of a two-year depression for Wendy.

On July 4, 1997, the extended families of both Fred and Wendy spent the holiday with Jaime, celebrating Independence Day. On July 10 Wendy visited her daughter at the foster home, held her hand gently, and told her, "I love you."

The next morning Jaime died peacefully in her sleep.

"It wasn't until then that we saw God's plan in taking Jaime to the foster home," Fred said. "It was the first time I had ever seen God deliberately step in and intervene in response to a direct prayer. We needed that two years to prepare us for her leaving permanently. He let us see that part of His plan. We just had to make the choice to allow God to work out His plan."

Adds Wendy, "We're also grateful that God allowed us to see what's coming down the road with Joel. So with him, I'm making every minute count. I'm praying he goes in the same peaceful way his sister did."

A MIRACLE CHILD

Dave Jones and I have worked together for the past twenty years. Yet until a few years ago I didn't know much about the challenges his family faced as he grew up. The biggest reason for that is that Dave didn't really see them as "challenges" until more recently.

"I never thought I grew up in an unusual home," Dave says. "What got me thinking about this was Christmas 1994."

When he called his parents in Florida that year, he asked to speak with his sister, Linda. His mother put her on the phone and Dave heard a deep, burly voice say, "Merry Christmas, David! Ho, ho, ho! Merry Christmas!" Linda started cutting up and teasing him, and Dave finally asked her, "What did you get for Christmas, Linda?"

"I got underwear," she replied.

"Underwear?" he exclaimed. "That's a terrible Christmas gift!"

"Yeah, bad gift—underwear is a bad gift, Dave!" Then she started laughing and cracking jokes about underwear.

"What else did you get for Christmas?" Dave asked.

"I got a new doll baby," she said.

"Linda, you're awfully old and kind of big to be playing with dolls," Dave teased.

"Yeah, me a big girl now," Linda said, then began mimicking Santa Claus once more. Soon she tired of talking, dropped the phone, and walked away. A few moments later Dave's mother picked up the phone and said, "Dave, what in the world was that all about? What were you two talking about?"

"Well, Mom, I see you're still buying people underwear for Christmas," Dave said.

"I didn't buy anyone underwear," his mom insisted. "Your sister is teasing you. She's making fun of me."

After he hung up the phone, Dave said he felt "weird." He couldn't stop thinking about the phone call. For the next several days he replayed it over in his mind.

"It really struck me," Dave says. "Linda had walked to the phone when we were told she would never walk. She knew what a telephone was, and supposedly she was so severely retarded she would never be able to function. She knew she was talking to her brother, whom she hadn't seen in months. She knew it was Christmas, and she knew Santa Claus was not real, so she was making fun of him. She knew that giving underwear was sort of a family joke, that we all thought of it as a bad gift for Christmas, so she made fun of Mom.

"For the first time it really struck me that my sister is a miracle child. She'd been called a vegetable, useless, worthless. People thought we should discard her, said she wasn't supposed to live. Conventional wisdom said that this child was ineducable, that she would destroy a home—but, in point of fact, for years she had been the glue that held our home together."

Linda was born in 1960 in upstate New York, the third child and first daughter of Norm and Ruth Jones. Ruth had always wanted a girl.

"My mother was really excited when Linda was born," Dave said. "On a scale of one to ten, she was a clear ten. She had crystal-clear blue eyes, an infectious smile, and beautiful, thick blond hair. There was just something special about her."

A few weeks after Linda arrived, Ruth took her daughter to get her DPT shots. After the first shot Linda started screaming, literally turned green, and momentarily appeared to fall unconscious. Ruth grabbed her baby and rushed to the doctor. The medical staff tried to reassure Ruth that Linda's reaction was normal. "This is my third child, and I know what's normal!" Ruth insisted. "This is not normal." The doctor told her everything was fine and not to worry. A month later Ruth returned to the doctor so Linda could get her final DPT shot, and once again the baby reacted violently to the medicine. After that incident it seemed as if Linda was never quite the same.

Months later a pediatrician in Washington, D.C., diagnosed Linda with severe mental and physical problems. A second opinion concurred, and the message Ruth remembers hearing everywhere was, "There's no hope. No hope. No hope."

Linda had suffered serious brain damage, accompanied by severe physical handicaps that became more pronounced as she grew older. Though she was only six months old, the doctors diagnosed her with muscular dystrophy and either multiple sclerosis or cerebral palsy. (Years later it was determined that Linda had cerebral palsy and severe scoliosis in addition to her brain damage.) Doctors said the child would never walk, communicate, or function at any level. They said the severity of her handicap made her a vegetable and she wouldn't survive long. Ruth and Norm were encouraged to institutionalize her, because it was thought that introducing such a child into the home would be divisive, disruptive, and would likely destroy the family.

But Ruth would have nothing to do with such counsel. Instead she took the attitude that with God's help, with the family pulling and working together, they would never lack hope. "There's always hope, especially because of God's sufficient grace," she often said.

And in the coming years her stubborn belief proved true. Ruth taught her daughter how to walk by working with her every day for seven or eight years. In the same way Linda learned how to talk a little (although mentally she never got beyond the age of two). After years of struggle Linda also was potty-trained, and today she even helps dress herself—all activities the doctors said she could never manage.

"My parents always treated her as an equal member of the family," Dave says. "They never treated her like she was retarded. They didn't change anything about the way they behaved. Linda had a few chores, like helping set the table (which was disastrous at times). When my parents went out in public, they took Linda with us. For the first several years we had to carry her, because she couldn't walk. When we'd go to church, she'd come with us. The other four children would sit in the front row with Linda, and she was expected to behave. My parents didn't change their routine; they weren't embarrassed by her. I mean, she was strange-looking. She drooled. Sometimes she would behave in a way that would draw attention to herself. But my parents' attitude was, if other people can't handle it, that was too bad.

"In fact, my dad used to joke when people would say in a pious way, 'Norm, what's it like raising a handicapped child?' He'd say, 'Well, I have five children. Which one are you talking about?' "

As he grew up, Dave never considered any of this a crisis. It didn't seem unusual to him in the least; in fact, he thought every family dealt with similar issues. Even when it came to death.

Several times Dave almost lost his sister. At age thirty she underwent major scoliosis surgery, and doctors warned the family that Linda might not survive. But they were wrong again, and a few months ago Linda celebrated her thirty-eighth birthday.

"My dad figures she'll outlive all of us," Dave says cheerfully.

THE JONES PRINCIPLES

What enables a family not only survive such a challenge but thrive through it? Before we get to my own take on this, I'd like you to consider ten principles that Dave says enabled his family to grow through Linda's physical and mental challenges.

1. A situation is a crisis only if a person lacks sufficient resources and grace to go through it.

Both of Dave's parents took the attitude that what had happened with Linda was not a crisis, that there was a purpose for it, and that God's grace was sufficient to get them through it. They loved the verse "My grace is sufficient for you, for my power is made perfect in weakness" (2 Corinthians 12:9).

They never wallowed in self-pity or asked, "Why did this happen?" or say, "Lord, turn back the clock. Make this problem go away." Instead, they said, "Okay, we've got an unusual situation to deal with. Let's trust the Lord that He will supply our need for this situation and will give us sufficient grace to deal with it."

2. Know God's Word. Meditate on it, because it has the power to equip you to overcome any situation.

Dave's parents were in love with God's Word. They didn't have to learn principles of coping when the crisis hit.

"I think that's why, growing up, I never thought of this as a crisis," Dave says. "It wasn't until I was forty-one that I suddenly thought, *There's something unusual here.* Until then it never occurred to me that it was a big deal."

3. If we wait until a crisis to pray, then when we need God the most, we will know him the least.

Prayer must be our first line of defense, not a last resort. Prayer always played a big role in Dave's family, so when the "crisis" did come, they were ready for it.

4. Put your roots deep into a Christ-centered local church.

Wherever Dave's family lived, his parents always immediately put roots down into a local Bible-believing church. After Linda was born, they became even more active. They didn't become introverted, lock themselves in their home, or get embarrassed to be in public because of their odd-looking daughter.

In fact, Dave says, "It was a Wednesday when my parents got the final word on Linda's condition. That night they went to prayer meeting like they did every Wednesday, and when they mentioned their news, the church held a special prayer meeting for them and their daughter. That's love. That's a support group."

5. God chooses what we go through in life, but we choose how we will go through it.

Ruth had been a music major and teacher, a recording artist, and a concert performer. When Linda was born, she put her career on hold and determined to take care of this child, help this child, do everything she could for this child. She loved a quote by author Chuck Swindoll: "Life is ten percent stuff, and ninety percent how we respond to that stuff."

6. Guard your heart.

Ruth knew that it wasn't what happened to her that counted, but what happened *in* her. Any normal human would look at this situation and say, "This isn't fair!" It would be very easy for someone in such circumstances to become bitter. Some people even said, "Ruth, you have a right to be bitter." But she always considered bitterness a sin and never allowed herself to be devoured by it.

7. Build your home and family on the foundation of the Lord Jesus Christ.

Trivial issues and trite agendas can't survive long in a family with a severely handicapped person. Norm and Ruth built their home on a solid faith in Jesus Christ, and it was that faith that allowed them to turn inside out the "conventional wisdom" that said Linda would create major dysfunction in the home and should therefore be institutionalized. In fact, her presence created unity, not dysfunction.

8. Do not disrupt relationships with other Christians.

No one is an island. You must have intimate friendships with individuals to whom you are accountable. Norm and Ruth never changed how they entertained or related to friends. They continued to invite people over to the home. And if these visitors couldn't handle Linda, that was their problem. They never apologized for her.

9. Keep an outward focus on life, a servant's heart, and a passion for people.

Norm and Ruth remained very active in the community despite Linda's disabilities. In addition to working with several Christian ministries, they kept an outward focus on life and found ways to serve others. They determined that one of their great goals was to please God, and they believed they did this best by obeying Him and by serving others.

10. Be imitators of Christ.

Norm and Ruth read the Gospels and observed how Jesus interacted with His Father, His friends, family, and others. Then they tried their best to imitate what they saw.

Norm tells how one night after a men's volleyball game he was riding home with Curly, a friend from church.

"You will never know how much your daughter Linda has influenced my life," Curly said.

"Curly, how can a severely handicapped, mentally retarded girl influence your life?" Norm asked.

"I've seen how you, Ruth, and your other children accept and love Linda, and that has given me courage, faith, and hope to deal with some of my own personal problems in a God-honoring manner," Curly replied.

A FEW KEY TRUTHS

Let me repeat something I said at the beginning of this chapter. It is not easy to explain why children are sometimes the victims of extreme suffering. I don't have the full answer to where God was when a child is born mentally and physically handicapped. I confess I don't fully understand his purposes. But I am convinced of a few truths:

1. The destiny of such children is assured by the work of Jesus Christ.
I believe that mentally retarded children incapable of making spiritual choices (such as Jaime and Joel and Linda) are automatically taken care of through the work of Christ. We will see them in heaven, at that time whole and healthy and happy.

As Wendy Bass says of her late daughter, "I so look forward to heaven! I really, really want to see Jaime whole. It could happen tomorrow and I wouldn't care. To see her talking and running and laughing—that will be heaven! And that's very different from how I viewed heaven before."

2. Despite any physical or mental handicap, all children are precious and made in the image of God.
In the Old Testament the psalmist declares to God, "You created my inmost being; you knit me together in my mother's womb. I praise you because I am fearfully and wonderfully made; your works are wonderful, I know that full well. My frame was not hidden from you when I was made in the secret place. When I was woven together in the depths of the earth, your eyes saw my unformed body" (Psalm 139:13–15).

Mental and physical handicaps do not invalidate a person's worth or status as one made in God's image.

3. God Himself explicitly honors people with handicaps.
One of the most amazing verses in the Old Testament is found in Exodus 4:11, where God says, "Who gave man his mouth? Who makes him deaf or mute? Who gives him sight or makes him blind? Is it not I, the LORD?"

His point is that He makes all people, regardless of their abilities or disabilities. He loves them equally and claims them equally as His special creations.

4. Some disabilities may occur to show the world something good about God.

In the ninth chapter of John's Gospel, Jesus is asked about a man born blind, "Rabbi, who sinned, this man or his parents, that he was born blind?" Jesus replied, "Neither this man nor his parents sinned, but this happened so that the work of God might be displayed in his life."

Jesus then healed the man and used his wounded life in an astonishing way to show the crowd something wonderful about God. God loves people, and He will use any means available— including blindness and other disabilities—to gain the world's attention and point them to His overwhelming love and power.

Something along those lines has happened with Fred and Wendy Bass. While Jesus didn't heal either of their two children, He has used their affliction to proclaim to fascinated observers the love of God and the hope to be found in Christ.

Shortly before Jaime died, Wendy was asked to write a letter to her daughter that would appear in *Letters to Our Daughters,* a book sold around the world. In part, that letter said:

> Dear Jaime,
> As I write this letter to you, you've just graduated from high school. Normally, this is a milestone in life when a mother reflects back on all that she has taught or hoped to impart to her daughter and prepares to give advice for the future. But, then, our lives have been anything but normal, huh, sweetie? For us I think it's the opposite; instead, it's how much you have taught me in 18 years.
> . . . Being our firstborn, we did not immediately recognize problems with your development. But it was a gradual process of acceptance, of letting go of dreams, goals, expectations, and learning to trust God for your future. You taught me that, Jaime.
> You taught me about perseverance and how to be an advocate. . . . You taught me how to be assertive yet to get along with others in the process. You taught me pa-

tience, a very hard lesson that I'm still learning—waiting on test results, waiting for any small sign of progress from hours, days, and years of working on skills in school and therapy. You taught me the value of what is really important in life. It wasn't my preconceived ideas of an orderly, successful, "happy" family, perfect as I could make it. But instead I learned the value of investing in lives, something that matters for eternity. . . .

You have touched so many people's lives, just being you. People have developed more compassion and acceptance and tolerance by being a part of your life, especially me. Those who have taken time to get to know you have come to love you, your social nature, your smile, your infectious laughter. They also cry for you when you are in pain, having your uncontrolled seizures, losing your eyesight. You have taught me joy for the little things and appreciation and thankfulness for things that are often expected or taken for granted. For many years you could not show love in return. What a joy and blessing it was to experience the first hug from you at age five, or your first attempt at a kiss at age 16. I have learned to live with adversity and to find a measure of happiness in that. I have learned to face the pain of inadequacy, not being able to fix things for those I love.

. . . I am so thankful to have had the awesome responsibility and privilege to care for and raise you for 18 years. I would not have traded it for an easier path, for you have taught me what is most important in life.

You will always be my little sweetheart.
Love, Mom

The May before Jaime died, she and Wendy appeared on a nationally syndicated TV program called "Caryl and Marilyn." Just before airtime Jaime grew agitated, and the show's producer thought she wouldn't be able to be on the program. But Wendy and some of the show's other guests prayed, and five minutes before taping began, Jaime calmed down and was a "perfect angel" for the five-minute segment. "She got to share her story with millions of people who also desperately need hope," Wendy said. "She went out with a bang."

That's the way God does things. While He never does evil, He can take even tragedy and use it for good. He does not forget us; sometimes He uses these terrible hardships to bring about other good.

5. Every life is a full life, no matter how long it is.

We think we have a right to eighty strong, healthy years; God says, "I made this life. I know what kind of life I have planned for every person." God looks at our life with eternity's perspective and has something much greater in mind for us—uncounted years in perfect happiness. Every life is a full life, whether it is six weeks, six years, or sixty years. It's a full life from God's perspective.

6. Handicapped children often bring out of others a unique tenderness and compassion.

Some of the tenderest, most compassionate, most sacrificial acts you'll ever be privileged to see are directed toward severely handicapped children. This may be one way God forces us to be tender in a hard and harsh world, on a planet indifferent to human weakness.

7. Severely handicapped children teach us that service delights God's heart.

We modern Westerners tend to detest the idea of serving someone else, although in fact we're all serving one another in one way or another. Even Jesus said of Himself, "The Son of Man came not to be served, but to serve, and to give his life as a ransom for many" (Matthew 20:28).

God is trying to teach us that we need each other, that in a fallen world service and sacrifice are part of living. I think the closest picture we have to the divinity and work of Jesus Christ is someone who dedicates his or her life to taking care of an incapacitated person.

Author Henri Nouwen spent years of his life taking care of a severely disabled man named Adam. An outsider who greatly admired Nouwen's writing once told him what a tragic waste it was that the author spent so many years of his valuable life caring for a mentally retarded invalid who could never give anything back. "You don't understand," Nouwen replied gravely. "I get far more out of my humble service than you could possibly know."

People who take care of others out of love become a model of what Jesus Christ did for us. Why was Mother Teresa so honored? Because even the most cynical among us could somehow see in her the Spirit of Christ. She pictured for people the unmerited love of God toward all of us.

8. Handicapped children force us to see our own frailty.

None of us are sufficient without God. Handicapped children tend to make us realize how dependent we are on God even for good health. As the apostle Paul once told the proud Athenians, God "himself gives all men life and breath and everything else" (Acts 17:25). Seeing the frail condition of the severely handicapped ought to make us grateful for every day of health that we do enjoy. It's a great mercy that so many of us do enjoy strong, healthy bodies.

9. Handicapped children expose the dark and wicked side of human nature.

Many of us consider any physical handicap a thing of derision, and we judge handicapped people as inferior. Somehow we tend to equate human beauty and strength with moral qualities. It has often been proven that good-looking people—handsome men and pretty women—get paid more, find better positions, and have greater access to positions of power.

Perhaps God brings severe handicaps into our lives to make us think, *Is this what life is all about? A pretty face? A well-placed pair of eyes? Is a tall, athletic, muscle-bound young man really superior to the brilliant physicist Dr. Stephen Hawking, who sits in a wheelchair and communicates only through his computer?* This may be one radical way that God makes a fallen, rebellious race rethink what we value. What is life all about?

I believe this is part of what the author of Ecclesiastes meant when he wrote, "It is better to go to a house of mourning than to go to a house of feasting, for death is the destiny of every man; the living should take this to heart. Sorrow is better than laughter, because a sad face is good for the heart" (Ecclesiastes 7:2–3). Why is it good for the heart? Because it brings you down to the basic fundamentals. It strips you to the core of what is human.

Inside a man or woman whose mental and physical capacities are diminished is a real human being with a soul and spirit, a person who is going to live forever. And he or she may understand even now much more than we imagine. When people in long-term comas finally awaken, they often describe in detail the conversations and activities that swirled around them as they lay still and silent on the hospital bed.

I recall a story about a young man who had been called a vegetable from the day he was born. Two nurses took care of him for many years. One always talked to him as she cleaned and fed and cared for him, and usually squeezed his limp hands as she prepared to leave the room. The other nurse performed her duties as hurriedly and impersonally as possible, resenting the fact that she had to spend any time at all on a man who could not so much as follow a visitor with his eyes. The man never responded even slightly to either nurse—until the loving woman reported one day that she would be moving away and would not be back again. As she turned to the man to say good-bye, she saw a single tear coursing down the man's cheek. And she knew he had understood all along.

In heaven we may discover that the severely mentally handicapped understand a great deal more than we think they do. It's an awesome thought.

10. Handicapped children may force us to think about our Creator.

Why is it that we sometimes can be so indifferent to God—until tragedy strikes? Just this past week I received a letter from Alison. Now, I love hearing from individuals from all around the world. But it's not every day someone wakes up and decides, "Today I'm going to write to Luis Palau."

Until recently, Alison and her partner ran their own business, which they had to give up after running into financial difficulties. On top of all that, Alison has an eight-year-old son with Down's syndrome and leukemia, and a six-year-old daughter who for the past few months has been asking Mom to tell her all about heaven and God. Alison finally realized she had no answers for her own life, let alone for her daughter or son. So the other day Alison went out and bought my book *God Is Relevant* and has since started writing via e-mail.

Alison admits she never would have thought much about God, however, if all of this hadn't happened—especially her son's desperate condition and her daughter's persistent questions. I think the same is true for many individuals. We're quite content, as Alison puts it, to ignore God while life is trolling along pretty well—until we're suddenly confronted with the seriousness of our child's condition. Perhaps God knows it's the only thing that will wake us up spiritually.

LINDA'S SURPRISE

Sometimes when we're busy asking "Why?" God is busy assembling a "Wow!" Dave Jones tells such a story involving his sister, Linda:

> When Linda was in her twenties, my parents were able to enroll her in a special school for mentally handicapped children only a few miles from their Florida home. In February 1980, shortly after Linda's thirtieth birthday, she became a full-time resident of the school, where she could be with other adults like herself. But even then my dad had the attitude that "we're still a family, and as a family we go together to church on Sunday." That was always a nonnegotiable in our home.
>
> Arrangements were made every Sunday for a family member, friend, or someone else to take Linda to church. Linda was always excited about being with her family and going to church. She would always return to her school eager to teach her roommates some song she had learned. Soon Linda's two roommates got very jealous. They didn't like it that she got to go to church and they didn't. So my dad and another man convinced the church it

needed to form a special-education class for mentally handicapped people within the Sunday-school program.

One day a social worker told my dad she didn't think it was a good idea to allow Linda and her roommates to go to church—it created jealousy among the other residents.

My dad replied that the church had a bus that should be able to transport the entire school to church. After a series of discussions and negotiations, school officials agreed that if the church would set up a special Sunday-morning program for these handicapped adults, the school would send two large vans full of residents to church each Sunday.

The church had a large, growing congregation with multiple services, and most members were unaware of the program for adults like Linda. One Sunday my wife, Gail, and I were visiting my family in Florida. As we sat in the worship service, suddenly from a side door, stage left, some forty to fifty mentally handicapped people started marching into the sanctuary. It was right before the morning message. I looked around, first at the choir, and saw looks of horrific shock as worshippers stared at these extremely handicapped people. I watched as a Sunday-school teacher and a couple of social workers tried to get all these disabled adults to line up in front of the podium. It seemed like an eternity, but the workers finally got everyone lined up and calmed down. Suddenly one of them grabbed his crotch and yelled, "Oh, no! Got to go to bathroom!"

The man bolted from the platform to head out the side door, a social worker chasing after him. After several more minutes the workers again managed to get everyone calmed down and lined up.

And then the most amazing thing happened. Suddenly they all started singing, "Jesus loves me, this I know, for the Bible tells me so." Remember, most of these people could hardly talk. And the joy in their faces! They were so proud and beamed from ear to ear. It was incredible. Such joy. Such enthusiasm. It was one of the most beautiful musical numbers I have ever heard.

I looked up at the choir, and where before I had seen horrific looks of shock—This is disgusting! Whose idea was this to *bring these retarded people in here?—there wasn't a dry eye in the loft. People sobbed openly. Others, with tears streaming down their cheeks, were mouthing the words, "Jesus loves me . . ."*

We found out later that my sister—this brain-dead, can't-survive, incredibly handicapped young lady—had taught her friends how to sing "Jesus Loves Me." Linda had learned the song years before from listening to my mother play and sing it at the piano. In fact, "Jesus loves me" were some of the first words Linda ever learned to speak. And now, years later, she had taught the same words to her group of handicapped friends.

Why does God allow children to be born with severe mental and physical handicaps? It's a question I doubt we'll ever be able to answer fully on this side of heaven. But I have another question that I think needs to be answered: Why don't we learn from Linda and her friends that the biggest question isn't "Why?" but "Who?"—and that the answer is Jesus Christ?

Do you have the assurance in your own heart that Jesus loves *you?*

The Bible tells us, "For God so loved the world that he gave his one and only Son, that whoever believes in him shall not perish but have eternal life" (John 3:16).

The Bible also tells us, "God demonstrates his own love for us in this: While we were still sinners, Christ died for us" (Romans 5:8).

It tells us, "This is love: not that we loved God, but that he loved us and sent his Son as an atoning sacrifice for our sins" (1 John 4:10).

Jesus himself tells us, "Greater love has no one than this, that one lay down his life for his friends. You are my friends if you do what I command" (John 15:13–14).

What is Jesus asking of me and you? That we open our hearts to receive His love and thereby receive the forgiveness of our sins, eternal life, and fellowship with Him forever.

"But how, Luis?" you may be asking.

I suggest that you pray the following prayer of commitment:

"Lord, I come before You humbly, in the midst of my heartache and

sorrow. Yes, please forgive my sins. Thank You that Jesus died on the cross to cleanse my heart and rose again to give me new eternal life. Thank You that now I can enjoy the sure hope of heaven. Please keep my precious little one in Your dear care. I love You and will live for You all the days of my life. Amen."

If that's your prayer, you, too, can sing![1]

[1] If you've just committed your life to Jesus Christ, please write to me. I'll be glad to correspond with you and send you a free copy of my book, *Your New Life with Christ*. It's yours free for the asking. Or maybe you would like to request prayer for your child. Again, please feel free to write. My address is Luis Palau, P.O. Box 1173, Portland, Oregon 97207, U.S.A. E-mail: palau@palau.org.

4

HOME,
SOUR HOME

F amilies are meant to nurture their sons and daughters in a healthy, safe environment, far from the frightful horrors haunting filthy alleyways in the seedier parts of town. But these days that's often not what happens. Increasingly we hear of dysfunctional homes in which abuse is the rule, not the exception.

Domestic abuse and violence scar hundreds of thousands of individuals each year. Perhaps someone you know has suffered in this way.

On a spring night I received an anguished call from twenty-seven-year-old Mary. She had been married twice and at the time of the call was separated from her husband.

"I have this thing that's been bothering me for many, many years," she said. "I was sexually molested by two of my brothers, and that has affected my relationship with the men I've been married to."

Her father, a minister who had died a few years before, never knew of the abuse, and the news devastated her mother when Mary finally told her about it. Mary couldn't remember when the violence started, but it ended when one brother got married and the other left to join the Navy. The last time it happened, she was nine or ten.

"It's affected me real bad," Mary told me. "It affects my relationships with my husbands, and now it looks like I can't even have children because of it."

I wish I could say that Mary's experience is exceptional, but I've heard stories like hers too many times to believe they're uncommon. The night before I spoke with Mary, I met another woman whose half-brother had abused her. Although she had been married for many years to a "fantastic" husband, she wept as she described her long-ago ordeal. She felt just as Mary did. Almost every woman I know who was abused as a girl goes through a similar experience.

Domestic abuse is so contrary to God's plan, so wrong, so out of order. In my opinion abuse in the home is one of the worst sins. It's despicable, loathsome, and an utter abomination. It is a horrendous sin. God designed the home to be a refuge from danger, a center for love and nurture. When instead it becomes a pit of betrayal, God is both hurt and angered.

I have taken many calls from women devastated by bitterness and rage who wonder how (or even why) they should forgive their abusive fathers. Other women have tearfully described how their brothers took turns using them for debauched sex. And many of them wonder: Did God not see these horrors? If He saw them, why didn't He act to stop them? Where was He when these unspeakable acts of violence were taking place?

A DIFFICULT SIN TO "EXPLAIN"

This is one of those sins that I find so hard to "explain." How can a father rape his own daughter? How can brothers or uncles or close family friends abuse the little girls who trust them? Incest horrifies me; how could it do otherwise?

This sin spreads its venom far beyond the innocent ones whose flesh is torn by its jagged fangs. Years later, the spouses of these victims often become "secondary victims." For reasons unknown to them, the exciting sexual relationship they had so desired simply goes flat. When somehow they learn that an uncle or brother or other trusted friend abused their spouse long ago, they also discover that, in a sense, they have been raped as well. For they, too, still pay for this ugly, despicable sin. And so do their children. Often a seemingly endless cycle of dysfunction is set in motion by a single wicked act.

Of course, little girls aren't the only victims of domestic abuse. In our increasingly perverted society, the circle of violation grows ever wider and more depraved. A few nights ago on the local news I heard that police had arrested a convicted pedophile after they discovered he had been molesting his eighty-seven-year-old father for the past dozen years. I'm quite certain I don't want to know any details.

We seem to inflict the most profound evil upon the ones who should be dearest to us. The ones we should protect the most, we hurt the most deeply. And this depraved behavior runs through all levels of society, from the most sophisticated social circles to the least, from the suburbs to the slums. Human depravity comes from the heart, and neither money, education, family background, or social position can banish its evil. It is not merely the "lowborn" who suffer in abusive homes; in fact, I find that it is often the wealthiest and most "sophisticated" who sink to most profound depths. I don't mean that the wealthy are intrinsically more prone to this evil than others; I simply mean that wealth enables the human heart to more fully express its evil. When your soul is satiated and you can afford to pay for anything, watch out!

But whether the abuse occurs in wealthy homes or poor ones, the devastation it inflicts can grow beyond description. On a spring night a couple of years ago I received a call from fifteen-year-old Luke. Despite his few years, he had already attempted suicide many times.

"I've had many problems with school, and I've also had a lot of family problems," he told me. "I've tried killing myself a few times, and I just can't stay at home. I tried to take my life because I have no friends. My mom is alone, and I live with my dad. I don't get along with my stepmom either. We fight all the time. My real mom and I get along, but she wants me to stay with my dad, and he's kind of abusive."

Just a few days before I spoke with Luke, I received another phone call from New York. Sue, a divorcée who lived with her eleven-year-old son, described a similar dreadful scenario. "The other day my boy didn't come down for dinner," she said. "But since he often came in late, I didn't worry. When he didn't re-spond to my calls, I went up to his bedroom—and was shocked. He had wrapped a telephone cord around his neck and was trying to take his life. 'Why are you doing this?' I asked. 'All the troubles in our family would go away if I go away,' he said. 'It's better if I'm out of the way, Mom, and I leave you without myself.' "

That is the pit of despair, made doubly deep by being hewed out in the middle of a dysfunctional home. Thank God that our Lord knows how to lift us up out of this pit! As the psalmist says,

> I waited patiently for the LORD;
>> he turned to me and heard my cry.
> He lifted me out of the slimy pit,
>> out of the mud and mire;
> he set my feet on a rock
>> and gave me a firm place to stand
> (Psalm 40:1–2).

If you are thinking about taking your life, come running to Jesus and say, "Jesus, I'm so desperate. I'm so lonely. I want to take my life." Jesus says to you, "Don't take your life. That's the devil's plan. I gave my life on the cross for you. You don't have to take your life. I want to give you a new heart, a new life, and a new start. I love you, and I want to walk with you, right where you are."

But to lift us up "out of the slimy pit," Jesus has to take hold of our hand. We have to allow Him to get a real grip; a mere hand-shake won't do.

When Marie called "Night Talk," it was obvious her conscience was bothering her. A twenty-two-year-old unmarried mother of a three-year-old and a three-month-old, Marie told me that she hadn't believed in God when six years previously she "got to-gether" with her boyfriend (the father of her children). He pro-fessed to be a Christian and he took Marie to church. Now, she said, she believed in God—but it was hard to continue in faith with her boyfriend in jail for murder.

"He didn't do it," Marie insisted. "He's in there for murder, but he didn't do it."

"You're sure?" I asked.

"Positive," she replied. "I was with him."

"Well, if indeed he truly was a committed Christian," I said, "first, he shouldn't have joined himself to someone who doesn't know Jesus Christ. You know, that's one of Saint Paul's laws. He said, 'Don't marry an unbeliever because you're going to have clashes, you're going to have confrontations.' Christ and Satan cannot get along. Light and darkness don't mix. So somewhere along the line, your boyfriend obviously turned his back on God. He began to live with you instead of marrying you properly, and had children with you without being formally tied to you in love and in the eyes of the Lord."

"He asked me to marry him four times," Marie countered.

"And you refused," I said. "You're a tough lady, eh?"

"My parents have been married for twenty-five years, and they've always been unhappy. I've had a real rough childhood, and I didn't want to get married."

"What was rough about your childhood?"

"My dad was an alcoholic. He used to beat up my mom. She never divorced him, and she was always unhappy."

"Are they still living together?"

"They're still together, and they still hate each other. They don't trust each other, and they're always talking bad about each other."

What a miserable life. From a human perspective, it's not hard to see how Marie ended up as she did. And her story is repeated thousands of times throughout this troubled world.

I think of Zamica, age nineteen, who called the program because she wanted to change her life. She had her first child at sixteen, two years later gave birth to twins, and was pregnant again at the time of her call. Two different fathers were involved, neither of whom married her. As we talked, she admitted she'd been sexually molested at ages two and five by family friends and baby-sitters.

Or I think of Daneta, age seventeen, with one child already and another on the way. She told me she contracted gonorrhea from the nineteen-year-old father, who denied responsibility for everything. She lived alone and didn't know where to turn.

How does God relate to all this suffering? Where does a loving Creator fit in with a creation in so much pain? Where was God when Mary and Luke and Sue and Marie and Zamica and Daneta found themselves abused and hurt and in deep despair?

NINE POINTS TO CONSIDER

There are at least nine things I would like to say to someone who wonders, *Where was God when I was abused in my home?* This isn't a complete answer to the question, and I admit that much mystery remains, but I believe these nine elements can work together to provide understanding and hope.

1. The abuse was not your fault.

This was one of the first things I told Mary when she called looking for peace and healing. "Mary, you are not responsible for what your brothers did to you," I said. "You did not do it willingly. You were a victim in this case. You were a little girl, and it was not your fault."

Often the victims of abuse believe that they are somehow responsible for what others did to them. Sometimes the abuser himself makes this claim. But it is patently false. The abuser is the sole person responsible for the abuse, and the victim does not share in his guilt.

2. God has given us freedom of choice.

We are not robots. We are not prisoners of fate. God has given us the power to choose what we will do and how we will act, and we are free to make moral decisions. I believe that this freedom of choice is the highest expression of love an all-knowing God can give us.

But of course there are risks involved. We can see this even in the very human arena of parenthood. Most parents want their children to love them not out of fear but out of choice; there would be little satisfaction if love were coerced. But some children refuse to love their parents, regardless of what love is shown them. That is the risk of freedom.

It is the same way on a larger scale with moral freedom of choice. God allows us to choose what we will; but some people use their freedom to make hurtful and damaging decisions. We must be willing to accept the consequences that some people will use their freedom for evil.

The world reaps what it sows, and sometimes the innocent suffer because the evil choose to use their freedom in ways contrary to God's law. We cannot fairly blame God for this evil, because we would not want our freedom of choice taken away. There is a moral order; there is right and there is wrong. Some people cause pain to others or get themselves into trouble simply because they break the law. We can choose to jump off a ten-story building, but we are not free to choose the consequences of violating the law of gravity. Freedom of choice is a great gift, but it also entails great responsibility. And using it for evil can cause tremendous suffering. That is simply the way of things, hard as it is.

3. The human heart is deceitful above all things and desperately wicked.
Few things show the depravity of the human heart more graphically than abuse in the home. It is hard to imagine how an adult could stoop to such despicable behavior as beating or terrorizing or sexually molesting a child, but it happens. Far too often.

And the ugly truth is, the potential for such gross sin is within all of us. The Bible says that "all have sinned and fall short of the glory of God" (Romans 3:23). The Bible doesn't leave any of us out; it insists that all of us, without exception, have been stained by sin:

> *There is no one righteous, not even one;*
> *there is no one who understands,*
> *no one who seeks God.*
> *All have turned away,*
> *   they have together become worthless;*
> *there is no one who does good,*
> *   not even one.*
> *Their throats are open graves;*
> *   their tongues practice deceit.*
> *The poison of vipers is on their lips.*
> *Their mouths are full of cursing and bitterness.*
> *Their feet are swift to shed blood;*
> *   ruin and misery mark their ways,*
> *   and the way of peace they do not know.*
> *There is no fear of God before their eyes (Romans 3:10–18).*

Perhaps the most telling description of all for our fallen natures is found in the King James translation of Jeremiah 19:9, which reads, "The heart is deceitful above all things, and desperately wicked: who can know it?"

Every one of us has a deceitful heart deeply infected with sin. In God's eyes, even the best of us is "desperately wicked." That's hard for most of us to imagine. We think of abusers as "desperately wicked," but we don't see ourselves like that. Oh, we may have our faults, but we don't think we deserve to be labeled "evil."

Yet that's just what no less an authority than Jesus calls us: "If you, then, *though you are evil*, know how to give good gifts to your children, how much more will your Father in heaven give good gifts to those who ask him!" (Matthew 7:11). Most of us recoil from such a suggestion, but that doesn't make it any less true.

We ought to detest the evil acts of those who abuse others, but we should never forget that the same evil lurking in their hearts also infects our own. None of us is born into the world free of the dark side of human nature.

4. Don't blame God for somebody else's sin.

God is not to be blamed for the sins of others. Once we grant that He has given us a free will to choose our own course of action, we cannot in the next breath blame Him for the way in which some of us exercise that free will. If it was the husband who abused his children, he is squarely and one hundred percent to blame. Don't blame God, don't blame the abuser's mother, don't blame his youthful environment. Those excuses are invalid and unacceptable. Each of us is responsible for his or her own sin. As the ancient prophet Ezekiel wrote, "The soul who sins is the one who will die" (Ezekiel 18:4).

5. God is not the author of evil, but he is fully capable of bringing good out of evil.

In the Old Testament it is hard to find a more dysfunctional family than the clan of Jacob. Jealousy, lying, cheating, physical abuse, rape, murder, betrayal—it's all described in Genesis, the first book of the Bible. This family was a pitiful mess.

And yet it was a member of this family, a man who was physically abused and betrayed and sold into slavery by his own brothers, who later in life was able to tell those who so badly mistreated him, "You intended to harm me, but God intended it for good to accomplish what is now being done, the saving of many lives" (Genesis 50:20). And it was through this train wreck of a family that God, centuries later, brought into the world the Savior, Jesus Christ.

God cannot do evil, nor is He ever tempted by it (see James 1:13)—but He is very good at bringing good out of evil. As the apostle Paul wrote, "We know that in all things God works for the good of those who love him, who have been called according to his purpose" (Romans 8:28).

6. God can wipe clean troubling memories.

There is no question that someone hurt by domestic abuse faces an uphill battle to overcome the effects of that abuse. But I cannot agree with those who insist that a victim of abuse must simply learn to live with tormenting memories, to get by as well as can be expected. Such a depressing diagnosis no doubt applies to those who attempt to find relief apart from the limitless resources of God, but it is a denial of the Gospel itself to say that wretched memories must continue to haunt a person for the rest of his or her life. Thank God for the promise of 2 Corinthians 5:17, which says, "Therefore, if anyone is in Christ, he is a new creation; the old has gone, the new has come!"

I don't mean that by pronouncing the sacred syllables "God" or "Jesus Christ" a person is instantly and magically delivered from the enormous emotional scars of domestic abuse. But I do mean that real healing is possible through the power of God in the Gospel. And that's just what I told Mary the night she called.

I'd like you to understand this," I declared to her. "God can wipe out your crippling memories so they will seem like a movie that happened to somebody else. You don't have to live under this burden for the rest of your days. Because you can't go on like this forever, can you?"

"No," Mary replied.

"I want to tell you this," I continued. "When Jesus Christ really comes into your life and into your heart, He changes you."

I then gave Mary the promise of Hebrews 9:14, which says, "The blood of Christ, who through the eternal Spirit offered himself unblemished to God, [will] cleanse our consciences from acts that lead to death, so that we may serve the living God."

"You've had your failures; you've had two marriages," I continued with Mary. "So you've sinned against the Lord. He will forgive you. But that verse also says that He will help you to forget the memories of what those two dirty brothers of yours did to you. It says the blood of Jesus will clean your conscience from evil works—the evil works you've done and the evil works that those two brothers did to you—so that you'll be able to leave them forever in the past.

"You could begin again tonight, as if you were a girl who was never abused. You could literally start over. If you give your life to Christ, it will be as if you were a new woman. No, it's not *as if* you were a new woman; you *will be* a new woman. Even your thought life will change. The Bible says we receive the mind of Christ (1 Corinthians 2:16). You could be cleansed in such a way that you'll be a different woman.

"It's Jesus Christ who does this. Nobody else can do it. You can talk to me till kingdom come. You can seek counsel. You can take prescription drugs. All of it might help just a tiny bit—but it's only Jesus Christ who can make you a new woman. Would you like that?"

"I'll try," Mary replied. "But I've tried many, many, many times."

"It isn't what *you're* going to do," I explained. "You've already tried to be a different woman. No, it is *Christ in you* who will work in your heart and in your mind. It is Jesus Christ who will make you into a different woman."

This may sound like a fairy tale to those who have never experienced the power of God through faith in Jesus Christ. But it works. It's real. I've seen it many times myself through years of ministry. It is no fairy tale. It's what the Bible calls "Good News." And it's available to whoever will take God at His word.

"But how, Luis?" you may be asking.

The apostle John tells us, "Yet to all who received him [Jesus Christ], to those who believed in his name, he gave the right to become children of God" (John 1:12).

The apostle Paul adds, "the gift of God is eternal life in Christ Jesus our Lord" (Romans 6:23b).

In other words, God's Good News is a gift to be received. It's a matter of accepting His Son, Jesus Christ, as your own Lord and Savior.

Have you received the free gift of salvation yet? If not, why not stop right now, where you are, and in the quietness of your heart talk to God? You can place your trust in Him this very minute. The choice is yours.

You can talk to God using any words you wish, of course. I suggest that you pray the following prayer of commitment:

"Lord, I come before You humbly, in the midst of my heartache and sorrow. Yes, please forgive my sins. Thank You that Jesus died on the cross to cleanse my heart and rose again to give me new eternal life. Thank You that now I can enjoy the sure hope of heaven as a part of Your wonderful, eternal family. Please bring healing in my family here on earth. I love You, Lord, and will live for You all the days of my life. Amen."

If that's your prayer, congratulations!

Welcome to the family of God![1]

Then . . .

7. Forgive the one who hurt you.

Apart from the power of Christ, I don't know how anyone can forgive a perpetrator of domestic abuse. Yet I do know that forgiveness is a prerequisite for finding personal peace. And I know also that Jesus Christ gives us the strength and resolve to forgive from the heart those who have abused us—as long as we are willing to allow Him to work in our lives.

Bill Conard is a friend of mine who worked as a missionary for several years. He grew up in an irreligious home with an alcoholic, abusive father, a man who eventually abandoned his family. Bill became an angry young man who hated his dad for walking away. One summer some friends invited Bill to a Christian camp, where he got into all kinds of trouble and made no effort to hide his wild ways and curb his foul tongue.

One day he was walking by a cabin in which most of the coun-

---

[1] If you've just committed your life to Jesus Christ, please write to me. I'll be glad to correspond with you and send you a free copy of my book, *Your New Life with Christ*. It's yours free for the asking. Or perhaps you would like us to pray for you. Again, please feel free to write. My address is Luis Palau, P.O. Box 1173, Portland, Oregon 97207, U.S.A. E-mail: palau@palau.org.

selors and leaders were praying. As Bill passed by, he heard his name. "Change Bill Conard," the counselors prayed. "Lord, change Bill Conard."

The prayer startled Bill and took him aback. *Am I that bad that God would have these people pray for me?* he wondered. It got him thinking, and shortly thereafter Bill was converted to Jesus. He went to Moody Bible Institute, then became a missionary to Peru, one of the best I've ever met.

One day in Peru, when he was in his mid-thirties, Bill thought, *I have never forgiven my dad for what he did to us.* So on his next return to the United States Bill stopped at JFK International Airport in New York. He figured that his dad still lived in New Jersey, found him in the phone book, and made the call.

"Is this Mr. Conard?" Bill said.

"Yes, I am," said the voice at the other end of the line.

"I'm your son," Bill said. "I've just come back from Peru, and Dad, I have not loved you. I have hated you. I have resented you all these years for the way you treated Mom and the way you treated us. But, Dad, I've opened my heart to Christ. Dad, I forgive you—all the things you did to Mom and to us—because God has forgiven me."

At the other end of the line all Bill heard was sobbing. For three to five minutes without a break, the only sound crackling through the receiver was that of weeping. Finally Bill said, "Dad, are you still there?"

"I'm still here," replied the shaken old man.

"Can I come to see you?" Bill asked.

"Yes," came the response.

Bill got on a bus, made his way to his father, and embraced him. His dad wept, repented, and asked for forgiveness.

That is what can happen when you receive Jesus Christ as your Savior—even if your father or your mother abused you and you're rightly angry toward him or her. A man is not to beat or insult or demean his wife or children; it's the most despicable thing in the world. There is reason to be angry, but the Lord says, "Forgive whatever grievances you may have against one another. Forgive as the Lord forgave you" (Colossians 3:13).

That's how Christ changes us, from the inside out. And it all starts when we receive Christ.

8. Remember that all evil will one day be judged.

No one gets away with anything—not murder, not rape, not abuse. God has promised that the day is soon coming when all sins not covered by the blood of Christ will be judged. And from His perfect and holy judgments there will be no appeal and no escape.

Jesus said, "There is nothing concealed that will not be disclosed, or hidden that will not be made known. What you have said in the dark will be heard in the daylight, and what you have whispered in the ear in the inner rooms will be proclaimed from the roofs" (Luke 12:2–3). The apostle Paul talks about "the day when God will judge men's secrets through Jesus Christ" (Romans 2:16). And the apostle John paints a sobering picture of coming judgment:

> *Then I saw a great white throne and him who was seated on it. Earth and sky fled from his presence, and there was no place for them. And I saw the dead, great and small, standing before the throne, and books were opened. Another book was opened, which is book of life. The dead were judged according to what they had done as recorded in the books. The sea gave up the dead that were in it, and death and Hades gave up the dead that were in them, and each person was judged according to what he had done. Then death and Hades were thrown into the lake of fire. The lake of fire is the second death. If anyone's name was not found written in the book of life, he was thrown into the lake of fire (Revelation 20:11–15).*

But why does God wait until that day to mete out judgment? No doubt the biggest reason is given to us by the apostle Peter: "The Lord . . . is patient with you, not wanting anyone to perish, but everyone to come to repentance" (2 Peter 3:9). God doesn't want anyone to die in their sin—not you, not me, and not even abusers. And so He withholds his hand of judgment until the end.

Jesus explained that God's strategy is like that of a farmer who discovers that an enemy has scattered weeds among the farmer's wheat. Rather than risk pulling up the wheat along with the weeds, he tells his workers to wait until the harvest. At that time the wheat is to be cut and placed into barns, while the weeds will be plucked up and burned. As Jesus says,

> As the weeds are pulled up and burned in the fire, so it will be at the end of the age. The Son of Man will send out his angels, and they will weed out of his kingdom everything that causes sin and all who do evil. They will throw them into the fiery furnace, where there will be weeping and gnashing of teeth. Then the righteous will shine like the sun in the kingdom of their Father. He who has ears, let him hear (Matthew 13:40–43; see also Matthew 13:24–30, 37–39).

9. Would it be a good thing for a rebellious world to enjoy continuous comfort?

I think we can carefully ask another question: "What if God protected every rebel from every evil thing that could touch him or her in a fallen world? Would anyone ever turn to Christ? Or would we all perish, comfortably, in our sin?"

I wonder: Would it be a good thing to live as fallen people in a fallen world, separated from God, and yet enjoy life as if we were in paradise? Would anyone ever come to grips with their sin? Or would we all die without Christ and spend eternity in hell?

Maybe a small illustration would help. Do you think it would be a good thing to have a body full of a curable disease but suffer no symptoms? Would it be a good thing to feel great right up until the day you died—when the disease could have been cured and you could have lived fifty more years? I don't think so. And neither do I think it would be a good thing to live in a fallen world that didn't show some signs of its fatal illness.

Please, don't misunderstand me. I am *not* saying that abuse of any kind is a good thing. It's not! It's horrible and despicable and completely inexcusable. But it happens in a fallen world, and if God can redeem any of that pain to lead someone to Christ, that is worth celebrating. Just as the pain of cancer is not a good thing in and of itself but may provide a good service if it leads to early detection and eradication of the disease, so the pain of abuse is not a good thing in and of itself but may provide a good service if the pain leads people to place their faith in the Great Physician, Jesus Christ.

GOD SPEAKS IN CHICAGO

Not all of those who call "Night Talk" end up speaking with me on the air. Many callers converse instead with trained counselors and staff workers. One of these callers spoke with my son Andrew.

Gloria attended our crusade one night with her parents and other family members. She told Andrew, "I felt God speaking to me. Your dad talked about women being raped as children, about being abused as teenagers, about being abused as adults. I suffered through all three of those."

When the invitation was given that night, Gloria didn't feel she could go forward to accept Jesus Christ because she thought that it would offend family members. But she returned the following Sunday night and spoke with a counselor named Gretchen, who led her to Christ.

Gloria told Andrew, "When your dad opened up the meeting that night, he looked at the crowd of only five hundred people and said, 'We wonder if we should have had this service tonight.' "

Then she stopped and said emphatically, "You tell him that, for me, it was worth it all."

Abuse in the home is a horrible, inexcusable, despicable sin. But Jesus Christ is greater than every sin and every injury. And like the Great Physician He is, He heals all who come to Him in faith.

Even you.

• Most of this chapter has been addressed to the victims of abuse, but it's possible that a few perpetrators might also read these words. So to those abusers who want to turn from their sin and be forgiven, I offer the following four points:

1. Take total responsibility for your sin.
You committed this sin, and you must take full responsibility for it if you want to break out of an old cycle. When you do so, it can be the beginning of a solution. But until you do, you will continue living in a psychological morass that will cause you to act irrationally and sinfully and will

continue to fill you with guilt. Stay there and you will
never experience freedom.

The first step toward freedom is admitting, "I did this. I
am responsible for it, and no one else. My mother is not
responsible. My father is not responsible. My wife and kids
are not responsible. Society is not responsible. I sinned and
I alone am guilty."

*2. Don't blame demons and devils for your own sexual mis-
conduct.*

The Bible says that demons and devils can be blamed
for some things, but sexual misbehavior is not one of them.
Sexual immorality is a sin of the flesh, not of the devil. The
devil doesn't know anything about it, except maybe to
make it easier for you to fall into it. He blinds people to
their sin, and he also can put temptation in front of them.
But there is no way that you can say, biblically, "I have a
spirit of immorality." That kind of talk is unbiblical. "The
acts *of the flesh* are obvious: sexual immorality . . ." (Galatians 5:19). You can't blame the devil for sexual immorality.
So don't try.

3. Ask for God's help to overcome your sinful impulses.

When Jim called our program seeking help, he had been
married nine years. For the previous three years, however,
he had been separated from his wife due to his abuse of
their two daughters. What kind of abuse? I wondered. Jim
said he "hollered" at his family and put them down a lot;
also there had been sexual abuse. Jim was fifty-two years
old, and both he and his wife had been married previously;
he had three stepchildren and two adopted daughters. He
told me he was trying to reconcile with his estranged wife,
with little success. He also said that his church was involved in his rehabilitation and he was seeking pastoral
help.

"Sometimes I feel I just don't have the strength to be
the kind of person that my wife and children need me to
be," Jim said. "Sometimes I think this is going to go on for
a long time and we're never going to be together again."

After talking with Jim for some time I told him, "God has a psychotherapy all His own, and it involves our past, our present, and our future. In the past, what He does for us is to forgive our sins—and that's fundamental, through the death of Christ on the cross. In the present, He helps us to get a clean conscience and He cleanses our minds and our memories. Although we don't blank out our past, nevertheless it is so dealt with that we can leave it behind. We don't have to keep digging it up. Then He gives us a future without sin, without regret, and without pain."

I then talked about Galatians 2:20—"I have been crucified with Christ and I no longer live, but Christ lives in me. The life I live in the body, I live by faith in the Son of God, who loved me and gave himself for me"—and told Jim, "You have to deal with the evil tendency within you, which in your case seems to be directed toward sex and toward children. You have to deal with this deeply and come to the Lord and say, 'God, this is awful. This is greatly offensive to You. It is terrible. And the dark side of me, Lord, says that I am inclined that way from a twist of birth. But I hate my corruption and I do not want ever again to touch a child with sensuous intentions.' Now, that is a radical thing. That's why Paul says, 'I am crucified with Christ.' Galatians 5 says, 'Those who belong to Christ have crucified the flesh. . . .'

"In other words, before the presence of God, we have to do a radical self-surgery. God does the work, but we have to cooperate with Him. What you have to do—perhaps with another man your age who is more mature than you in the Lord—is to pray to God and say, 'Lord, I must deal radically with this sexual power within me. I don't have the power, but You do and You live in my heart. Lord, if I were on my own I'd probably stumble again, but I'm not on my own because Christ lives in me.' "

The word "radical" is exactly the right one here. Nothing else will do.

4. Don't allow yourself to play with pornography.
Most men seem more ashamed of pornography than

they are of adultery. The human mind knows it's a dirty deal. It attracts and intrigues through a surrogate sexual act, yet it is so destructive. A psychologist friend in Washington, D.C., told me that he counsels many men, even leaders, who are obsessed with pornography. They rent filthy movies and watch them for hours. The danger, he says, is that this sometimes leads them to act out what they watch.

An addiction to pornography can lead to extreme forms of perversion involving children or young girls. Many serial killers were pornography addicts. There seems to be a strong connection between twisted love in the home, pornography, crime, and violence. So don't get near the stuff. Ever.

5

In the Blink
of an Eye

The evening news report on November 8, 1994, shocked the nation. A Chicago family, heading to Milwaukee on Interstate 94, lost six of its nine children when a powerful explosion engulfed the family's van in flames.

A joint investigation by Milwaukee police and experts from the Federal Highway Safety Administration quickly determined that the fatal accident occurred when the van hit a trailer mud-flap unit lying in the middle of the freeway. The contraption penetrated the van's gasoline tank, causing it to explode and instantly kill five of the children.

At a news conference held eight days after the accident, the bereaved father, Duane Willis, described what happened.

"I was looking at the road and was alert," he said. "Our little baby was behind us; [our son] Ben was behind us on the other side. In the backseat were the other four children; they were all buckled in.

"I saw the object and thought it was one of those blocks that maybe came off one of those flatbed trucks. The car in front of me swerved, and I knew I couldn't miss hitting the object. I thought if

I took it on the tire, I might roll the car. It was a split-second decision.

"When we hit the object, the rear gas tank exploded, taking the car out of control. I was able to grip the wheel and take the car out of the slide. When we were sliding and the flames were coming around the seat, it was a shock—a surprise—like, 'What is this?' It was just roaring flames coming up on both sides. I was yelling to get out of the car. [My wife] Janet and I had to consciously put our hands into the flames to unbuckle the seat belts and reach for the door handles.

"Janet fell out the door while the car was still moving. Benny was in the midst of the burning; his clothes were mostly burned off by the time he got out. The five youngest children, who had been asleep, died instantly. No sound was heard by Janet or me as we struggled to get out of the van. An unknown man took his shirt off his back to soak Benny's wounds, and another beat out the burning clothes on Janet's back. Benny died in intensive care around midnight."[1]

All around the country and the world, people reacted to the story with disbelief and horror. How could it have happened? Such appalling accidents unfold so quickly and do their deadly work so thoroughly. Why doesn't God prevent them? How can He allow them? Does He turn His back when human beings become human torches?

Hard questions like that resurfaced again the morning of December 1, 1997, when fourteen-year-old Michael Carneal walked into Heath High School in Paducah, Kentucky, inserted earplugs, pulled out a semiautomatic pistol, and started shooting randomly at students who had just pronounced the final "Amen" at a group prayer session. Three girls were killed in the unprovoked attack—Nicole Hadley, fourteen; Kayce Steger, fifteen; and Jessica James, seventeen—and five others were wounded. One, Missy Jenkins, was left paralyzed.

Students later reported that the week before the shooting Carneal had warned "something big is going to happen" and had urged friends to skip the prayer meeting on the fateful day. Car-

[1] *How Could They Make It? The Willis Family Story* (Chicago: Parkwood Baptist Church, n.d.), 3, 4.

neal told a detective he didn't know why he shot his classmates and told a teacher, "It was like I was in a dream, and I woke up."[2]

When news of this horrifying event flashed around the world, many people began to wonder if God Himself had been asleep. How could He allow such a tragedy? And right after a prayer meeting! What sort of God could sit by and permit His own children to be murdered in cold blood?

A Planet of Tragedies

We live in a tragic world. No matter what your philosophy of life may be, regardless of what you may believe or disbelieve about God, I think we all can agree on one thing: Our planet suffers through its share of tragedies.

Fatal accidents. Senseless murders. Lifetime disabilities imparted in an instant. You don't have to look far to uncover sudden tragedies that change someone's life forever.

How does the God of the Bible relate to these tragedies? Where is He when they occur? Can we continue to believe in a loving God who would permit such catastrophes to happen?

These are good questions, and I would like to reply to them by suggesting the following six responses:

1. Accidents and even mayhem are a part of life in a fallen world.

The moment Adam and Eve disobeyed God in the Garden of Eden, they brought sin into the world—and deadly accidents and murderous acts soon followed. Cain, the very first human baby, grew up to become the very first human murderer (see Genesis 4:1–8). And accidents have plagued humankind ever since the race was driven from Eden.

No one is exempt, not even the most godly. I doubt that few would question that the apostle Paul was one of the most effective and dedicated Christian workers in history, yet his life was peppered with serious accidents until it finally ended under the blade of a Roman executioner. In one of his letters Paul sketched out a few of his hardships:

[2] "Three Kentucky High School Students Killed in Prayer Meeting Shooting," EP News Service, Vol. 46, No. 49, December 5, 1997, pages 1, 2.

I have worked much harder, been in prison more frequently, been flogged more severely, and been exposed to death again and again. Five times I received from the Jews the forty lashes minus one. Three times I was beaten with rods, once I was stoned, three times I was shipwrecked, I spent a night and a day in the open sea, I have been constantly on the move. I have been in danger from rivers, in danger from bandits, in danger from my own countrymen, in danger from Gentiles; in danger in the city, in danger in the country, in danger at sea (2 Corinthians 11:23b–26).

Paul suffered through at least as many accidents and hardships as any of us ever will, and yet their painful occurrence never shook his confidence in a good, loving God. Why not?

Unlike us, Paul did not see tragedy as *prima facie* evidence against the existence of a compassionate heavenly Father. In fact, he could write, "for Christ's sake, I delight in weaknesses, in insults, in hardships, in persecutions, in difficulties. For when I am weak, then I am strong" (2 Corinthians 12:10). Don't misunderstand; Paul was no masochist. He didn't delight in hardships and accidents because he enjoyed pain. No, he meant that when life overwhelmed him, he knew that God would step in to help. Paul delighted in his own "weakness" because it was that weakness that gave God the opportunity to display to the world His own irresistible strength. And for that Paul was grateful.

Jesus, too, told us to expect pain and difficulties in this life. "In this world you will have trouble" He warned His disciples in John 16:33. And to the public at large, He said this about the future: "Nation will rise against nation, and kingdom against kingdom. There will be famines and earthquakes in various places" (Matthew 24:7). It isn't a pleasant thought, but that's the way life is sometimes in this fallen world. It may shock us, but it shouldn't surprise us.

The Reverend Don Young is the pastor of Bible Baptist Church in Paducah, Kentucky, the church Nicole Hadley attended before she was gunned down that deadly morning at Heath High School. At a memorial service attended by more than four thousand people and watched by millions more on CNN, Pastor Young said to Nicole's grieving parents, "There's a question that begs to be answered, and I want to attempt to do so in these next two or three minutes. The question asked of me by kids, the question the media wants to know, the question that you want to know, is: *Why?*

"First, I'd like to share with you that my God didn't orchestrate your daughter's killing. I lost my own grandbaby, but God did not orchestrate that. I cannot serve a God who gives children cancer. You see, we're not puppets and God's not a puppeteer. He gave us something that He didn't give the animal kingdom. He gave them instincts; He gave us the power of choice. He made Adam and Eve, He put them in the garden, and He said, 'Serve me, if you will.' They chose to disobey.

"And last Monday morning, at least forty Heath High School students deliberately got up and made a choice—a choice that should be made by all American kids—a choice to exercise their right to communicate with their God. They walked in there, exercised their right of free choice, and bowed their heads. And another young man, for some unknown reason—once again, not orchestrated by God—ended three of their lives, and wounded five. He, too, exercised his power of choice."

Life follows such dark paths on a fallen planet like this one. It's tragic. Agonizing. Senseless. But, thank God, that is not where the story ends.

2. God is in control, even when it doesn't seem as if He is.

Events never spiral out of God's control, as if He somehow lacks the power or insight to direct the affairs of our little planet. That is why the apostle Paul, a man who knew intimately the pain of a fallen world, could tell the ancient Athenians, "The God who made the world and everything in it is the Lord of heaven and earth. . . . From one man he made every nation of men, that they should inhabit the whole earth; and he determined the times set for them and the exact places where they should live. God did this so that men would seek him and perhaps reach out for him and find him, though he is not far from each one of us" (Acts 17:24–27).

The Bible insists that God is sovereign: "His dominion is an eternal dominion; his kingdom endures from generation to generation. . . . He does as he pleases with the powers of heaven and the peoples of the earth. No one can hold back his hand or say to him: 'What have you done?' " (Daniel 4:34–35). Even when tragedies occur and innocent life is taken or maimed, God remains in ultimate control. Nothing happens that does not first pass through His loving hands.

We may not fully understand this when we face painful trage-dies, but our lack of understanding does not diminish or destroy its truth. Before we were born, God knew exactly how long we would live and how we would die. "All the days ordained for me were written in your book before one of them came to be," the psalmist said to God in Psalm 139:16. And that remains true whether those days are many or few.

3. God has a purpose in what He allows, even if we don't know what it is.

From our perspective tragedies look meaningless and senseless and chaotic, but God knows how to take even tragedies and bring good out of them. Although I do not believe that God causes all tragedies—the Bible says He is incapable of sin—I do believe that He has a purpose in allowing painful events to occur. Nothing that happens is a mad, meaningless accident. We may not understand what His purposes are, but we can take comfort in the fact that they exist. God specializes in taking evil and bringing good out of it.

At the memorial service for the three young women killed in Paducah, the Reverend Tom Hughes, pastor of Kevil Baptist Church, said to friends and relatives gathered that afternoon, "You might ask me, 'Preacher, do you really believe the words that you're saying? How has God been working, bringing forth blessing and good out of this?' God has already been working and bringing forth blessing and good because He has brought forth a greater quality of life in at least two individuals who have received organs from Nicole. God has already been working in these past few days; it has been brought to my attention that there are some students at Heath High School who, prior to Monday morning, did not know the Lord—but they know the Lord today."

Did the Lord cause these three young women to die so that the lives of two others could be spared and the souls of several others might be redeemed? No. God is not a murderer. But He does know how to take tragedy and bring good out of it. When we get home to heaven, we will finally see His purposes even in the tragedies of life. In the meanwhile, we must continue to believe that He does have a purpose in everything that happens—even if right now we are unable to see a shadow of what that might be.

4. Tragedy can serve as a wake-up call.

Oxford professor C. S. Lewis wrote years ago that "pain is God's megaphone to a deaf world." In that way some tragedies may serve as wake-up calls for spiritually sleeping people. A caller to "Night Talk" thought that might explain what had happened to him.

Bob, a twenty-eight-year-old self-confessed thief, liar, and fornicator, had suffered an accident at work. Somehow he had spilled hot wax in his eye, and he was afraid that his vision had been permanently impaired.

"I'm thinking that maybe this is kind of a punishment or a wake-up call for me to get my life in order," he said.

"I really appreciate the term you used—that it's a wake-up call," I replied. "Most of us are stubborn, and it seems as if God has to shake us up before we finally come to our senses and say, 'Hey, wait a minute. What's happening in my life?' These things make you think deeply about the ultimate issues of life. I suppose that may be what has happened to you in the last twenty-four hours."

A stubborn, secular, and even blasphemous society sometimes will be stopped short only when a tragedy of national proportions takes place. When the horror of it causes the media to pick up the story, sometimes redemptive truth gets out. That certainly happened in Paducah.

In a way, "tragedy" is a big reason that the cross and crucifixion of Christ still grip our imagination (even those who reject the Gospel). There is something so profound about Calvary that even people whose religion has nothing to do with Christianity, even people who reject Christ both intellectually and verbally, nevertheless are gripped by the story.

Thank God, perhaps, that He allows tragedy to so grab people. But what a shame that it takes such a horrendous wake-up call for us to open our sleepy eyes.

5. It is possible to embrace hope even in the midst of tragedy.

I cannot imagine what it would be like to endure a tragedy without the hope that God offers. Without Jesus Christ, there is no hope. There is simply an eternal, black, cold, and unrelenting void.

Author Tim LaHaye describes a debate he once had with an atheist. For two hours at an annual meeting of The American Humanist Association, LaHaye debated a forty-year tenured philosophy professor from UCLA on the existence of God. In an article published before the debate in the *American Humanist* magazine, this atheistic professor told about the tragic loss of a grandson who died from a birth defect before he reached three months of age. The professor described how he stood at the crib where the dead boy lay and cried out, "My son, you shall live as long as I live, for you shall live in my mind!"[3]

How pathetic. *That* is hope?

First, most of our memories die within a year; only infrequently do we remember something long-term. And second, if this is the best hope we have, it means that after your immediate family is dead, you're gone. Wretched thought!

Fans of the TV franchise "Star Trek" know the name of series creator Gene Roddenberry. What they may not know was that the late Roddenberry was an atheist whose beliefs sometimes colored the show's scripts. I think of one episode of "Star Trek: The Next Generation," in which the ship's security chief is killed off. At a memorial service for the slain officer, surviving crew members quote an old line from an Anglican funeral service: "with the sure and certain hope of the resurrection." Yet there is one big difference. The line in the show reads, "with the sure and certain hope that she will remain alive in our memories." I doubt that I've ever witnessed a flatter or more depressing funeral, make-believe or real.

When my twin sons were in high school, we received an announcement that some movies about death were scheduled to be shown in class. Administrators wanted parents to know about the films in case they wanted to come to school, view the movies, and then have something to talk about at home with their kids.

If I recall correctly, the film was titled *David Is a Memory*. The title character dies and becomes nothing but a memory. "Where is

[3] Tim LaHaye, *The Power of the Cross* (Sisters, Oreg.: Multnomah Publishers, 1997), 79, 80.

David now?" a boy asks. "Well, he's gone," he is told. "Yeah, but is he somewhere?" "No, he's a memory now. We will always remember him, and it will be wonderful, every time we think about him."

I found the film appalling, pathetic, and depressing. How far removed from the hope of the Gospel! Just last week I had a lengthy conversation with a cynical man who didn't believe in anything. What a miserable way to finish this life. I think unbelievers must, from time to time, wish that they had the hope of eternal life and a home in heaven. But of course, they have no such thing. Instead they have cynicism.

Of course, we Christians grieve when those we love are taken from us, but we do not grieve as those who have no hope. We do not believe that people cease to exist (except as memories) when they die; the Bible tells us that we will again see all those loved ones who put their faith in Christ. As the apostle Paul writes, "Brothers, we do not want you to be ignorant about those who die, or to grieve like the rest of men, who have no hope. We believe that Jesus died and rose again, and so we believe that God will bring with Jesus those who have died in him" (1 Thessalonians 4:13–14).

Thank God, some atheists come to recognize their hopelessness and turn from it. A distant relative of mine who for almost seventy years claimed to be an atheist came to me one day and said, "My dad was an atheist. I've always claimed to be an atheist. But now I'm reading the Bible and trying to get insights, and, Luis, if there's a God, I want to know Him. If there's eternal life, I want to have it. Can you help me?" At least he was honest, but he waited a long time to find the hope he lacked.

Sometimes the only thing that will move such skeptical people to faith in Christ is the death of a loved one through a tragic accident. Mandy's story is like that.

I first met thirteen-year-old Mandy following a youth rally outside London. She had never heard about Jesus Christ, but when she learned that Jesus died for her sins on the cross, rose again, and was coming back to take her to heaven, she invited Christ into her heart. Over the next several months Mandy told everyone she knew about what Jesus had done for her. She especially emphasized that she was going to heaven when she died.

Three years after our meeting I received a call from England that Mandy had been killed in a car accident three days before her sixteenth birthday. She had died instantly, and her parents wanted me to come to deliver the funeral message. "Mandy talked about nothing more than Jesus, Luis Palau, and going to heaven," they told me.

Mandy's death rattled the family, but especially her aunt and uncle. They had been atheists, and it took this horrible tragedy to prompt them to abandon their atheism and come to Christ. "In all your life as an atheist," I asked Mandy's uncle, "did you ever think about death and eternity and the meaning of life?"

"Only twice," he replied. "Once when I shot a bird with my rifle. My dad rebuked me, but not for the right reason, nor did I get a good lesson out of it. He said, 'Don't you ever kill a bird again. Look!' He forced me to pick up the bird, and it was stiff. For one fleeting moment I thought, *I wonder what happened? Five minutes ago this bird was alive and singing and flapping its wings, and now it's stiff*. But I missed it. Later a friend of mine was killed in a motorcycle accident, and for one fleeting, almost imperceptible moment, I thought, *I wonder where he is, if he's anywhere?* And then I dismissed it."

He didn't again consider the idea of life after death until Mandy was killed, and at that time he was converted to Christ.

Hope is readily available to all of us, even in the midst of tragedy. And not only hope for eternal life and hope of being reunited with those we love. Hope is available *right now*, square in the middle of tragedy, because God has promised to walk with us through any disaster that might overtake us.

As Pastor Don Young told the overflow audience at the Paducah memorial service, "Well, where in God's name does God come into this picture? I'm going to tell you where He comes in. When tragic and horrible and dramatic things take place, God says, 'I'll be there, I'll walk with you. When you walk through the valley, I'll walk with you. Though you walk through the very valley of the shadow of death, you need not fear evil. . . . You don't have to walk through death alone. I'll meet with you and I'll walk with you.' That's where God comes in."

6. This world is not our final home.

When loved ones die in tragic accidents or at the hands of wicked men, it is good to remember that this world is not our final home. At the funeral of a good friend just weeks ago I heard the officiating pastor say, "He is not now what he once was; he is in another state. He is himself, but he's in a much superior state." He meant that my friend Duane is no longer suffering as he had been. He is now with the Lord in heaven, and no pain or suffering or tragedy can ever touch him again.

We were created for eternity, and tragedy can never change that. This is only a transition period, a prelude to what God really has in mind for us. But because we usually look only at the present, we often consider someone's death premature or untimely. Our perspective is enormously limited. We tend to look only at what could have been (and in our minds, should have been) down here on earth. But God looks at all of eternity. If we are to cope with tragedy, we must learn to look at it through eternity's lens.

On "Night Talk" Chris called in to talk about his late brother. One night when Chris stayed home with his sister and three younger half-brothers, his brother died in a car accident. Two years later Chris was still struggling with the accident.

"I'm twenty-one; my brother was seventeen," he told me. "A cabdriver ran a yellow light and smashed right into his car, and the steering wheel crushed his head up against the roof. Until then we were pretty big with the church; we used to go every weekend and once during the week. My mother said, 'If your faith is strong enough, maybe a miracle will happen,' so I stayed with him in the hospital all week long while he was in a coma. I prayed every night at his bedside—and nothing came of it. Now my faith is gone."

I discovered that Chris's brother loved the Lord, so I focused on the hope of eternal life we Christians enjoy.

"If he loved Jesus Christ and believed in him with all his heart, you know the Bible says that he went to heaven when he died," I said. "Do you believe that?"

"At one time I did," Chris honestly replied.

"The great comfort is this," I continued. "The Lord Jesus said these words, 'You trust in God. Trust also in me. In my Father's house there are many rooms. I am going to prepare a place for you'

(John 14:1–3). The great difference between those of us who believe in Jesus and those who don't is that they have no hope. Accidents can happen to any of us, and we are all going to die, unless Christ returns first. We're part of a fallen race, and the punishment for rebellion is death. We're all condemned to die—but we can have eternal life when we put our faith in Jesus Christ.

"Chris, I can understand your frustration, and I fully believe the Lord understands your anger and confusion and desperation. Even though all of us know we will die, we all think we're entitled to seventy years. But when the Lord allows our life to be cut short, then we have to bow the knee and say, 'God, You are King of kings. I don't understand Your ways, but Lord, You are my God.'

"I know it's tough and we don't always understand the ways of God, but your brother is in the presence of the Lord. And one day, if you and your mom and the whole family trust Jesus Christ, you'll all be together in the presence of the Lord in the Father's house. We'll have a party that will never end!

"Chris, God has a plan for us that offers more than just life on earth. I encourage you to come back to the Lord and let Him take over in your life. Let faith be reborn in you and nail your faith to the Bible, to the Word of God—not to the word of men, not mine or anybody else's. Say, 'Lord, I really want to know You. I *have* to know You.' Hope will be reborn in your heart, and you'll begin to walk with God again. God says, 'Chris, I want you back, man.' As the Lord says in the book of Proverbs, 'My son, give me your heart' (Proverbs 23:26). The Lord would love to take you back and forgive you and restore you so you can walk with God again and enjoy His fellowship.

"The shock of losing your brother, whom you love so much, will never disappear completely, but you will be able to say, 'I will see my brother!' It's a promise from God who made us and loves us. You'll see your brother again, and you'll enjoy him. And never again will we die or suffer or cry."

This hope of heaven sustained the heart of Jessica James until the day she died. The Reverend Kelvin Denton, Jessica's pastor for ten years at the Kevil Baptist Church in Paducah, told those attending her memorial service that just months before she died, she wrote the following entry in her journal while at the tail end of a youth camp: "July 10. I thank You, Lord, for this week. Now I'm ready for You to come and get me. My bags are packed; my Bible is on my bags. Love You for eternity, Jess."

Then Pastor Denton looked at his audience and said, "If anybody was ready Monday morning, Jessica was. As a seventeen-year-old child, she understood what Jesus meant when He said, 'You must deny yourself and take up your cross and follow Me.' And Monday she followed Him all the way to heaven."

Confident to the End

Fatal accidents and the sudden, deadly assaults of men wrench our hearts and strike terror into our souls, but they needn't shake our confidence in a good, loving God. A few days after hearing the awful news about those six children killed in the Milwaukee van explosion, I was stunned to hear the reaction of the children's parents, Duane and Janet Willis. It wasn't what I expected—but it was exactly what I hoped my own reaction would be in similar circumstances.

"God is the Giver and Taker of life," they declared. "We must tell you that we hurt and sorrow, as you parents would for your children. The depth of pain is indescribable. The Bible expresses our feelings that we sorrow, but not as those without hope."

And where did they get this hope? They continued, "What gives us our firm foundation for our hope is the Bible. The truth of God's Word assures us that Ben, Joe, Sam, Hank, Elizabeth, and Peter are in heaven with Jesus Christ. We know, based upon the Word of God, where they are. Our strength rests in the Word of God. The Bible is sure and gives us the confidence. Everything God promises is true."

Wow! But then came the clincher: "God has prepared us for this trial. We're not special people. We're sinners saved by grace. But we're not taking a short view of life; we take a long view of life, and that includes eternal life. We realize that someday we'll stand before the Lord, and the things that are here will matter very little. God's grace is sufficient for everybody."[4]

From the lips of others those amazing words might sound trite and unconvincing. But these people are not talking about hypo-

[4] *How Could They Make It?* 5, 6.

thetical tragedies or theoretical catastrophes. They lived through one of the most horrific disasters imaginable, and yet they did not give up their faith in Jesus Christ. Much to the contrary, they leaned on Him as never before. And today they invite others to do the same.

How about you? Duane and Janet Willis published a booklet about their experience titled, *How Could They Make It?* In it they ask readers to consider the question "Am I prepared to handle the certainty of death?" And they ask, "When you stand before the Lord God, what will His decision be concerning you? Do you have absolute assurance that heaven is your eternal home? Have you trusted in Jesus Christ as your personal Savior from the penalty of your sins?"

Those are excellent questions. I wonder: How would *you* answer them?

Have you committed your life to Jesus yet? If not, why not stop right now, where you are, and in the quietness of your heart talk to God?

I suggest that you pray the following prayer of commitment:

"Lord, I come before You humbly, in the midst of my heartache and sorrow. Yes, please forgive my sins. Thank You that Jesus died on the cross to cleanse my heart and rose again to give me new eternal life. Thank You that now I can enjoy the sure hope of heaven. Help me to share that good news with others. I love You and will live for You all the days of my life. Amen."

If that's your prayer, congratulations!

Welcome to the family of God![5]

---

[5] If you've just committed your life to Jesus Christ, please write to me. I'll be glad to correspond with you and send you a free copy of my book, *Your New Life with Christ.* It's yours free for the asking. Or perhaps you still have questions. Again, please feel free to write. My address is Luis Palau, P.O. Box 1173, Portland, Oregon 97207, U.S.A. E-mail: palau@palau.org.

6

I'm Afraid I Have Some
Bad News for You . . .

A few weeks ago, in the midst of writing this book, I traveled to Southern California for the funeral of one of my best friends, Duane Logsdon. For the last nine years of his life Duane suffered from a rare form of cancer that inflicted excruciating pain on his body until the moment he died.

Duane said the pain in his ear was like the roar of a jet engine that never let up, day or night. He hardly ever slept.

"No, you don't get used to it," he told me. "And yes, it is roaring like a jet engine. And no, it never goes away. Never for a moment."

About three years into this horrific ordeal he told me, "Luis, I'll be honest with you. I have thought of suicide. That's how bad it is. But I rejected that plan because I know it's wrong. Still, I'm in agony—and it's worse knowing that this obviously is not going to go away."

Duane tried everything to find some relief from the pain, contacting every qualified doctor and exploring every promising new technique. He even tried a procedure used with U.S. Air Force pilots—but nothing helped. The roaring in his ear continued for nine long years until the instant he drew his last breath.

It makes you wonder, Where is God when good people like Duane suffer such intense pain from ghastly diseases? Is God in the doctor's office when you hear, "I'm sorry, but you have only a few months to live"? Or does He escape out the back door?

Larry was struggling with some of these issues when he called "Night Talk" from San Antonio.

"I'm going through hell, I don't know what to do anymore," he said through heaving sobs. "I'm thirty-two, I'm gay, and I'm dying of AIDS."

"Larry, I want to tell you something, my friend," I replied. "God loves homosexuals."

"If God loves me so much, why am I going through all this pain?" he tearfully asked.

It's a logical question and one we all tend to ask when illness and disease elbows its unwelcome way into our lives. Where is God when we learn we have terminal cancer or AIDS or any number of other excruciating maladies that cripple and kill us? If God really does love us, then why does He allow us to endure so much pain?

GOD'S PURPOSES IN
ALLOWING DISEASE

Before I give my response to the question "Where was God when this disease appeared?" I want to remind you that disease and death have always stalked the human race. This problem is not a new one, yet its persistence has never disproved the reality of a loving God. Throughout most of history God's people have accepted that illness and disease are a part of life on a fallen planet. They have understood that until the day God remakes this world and destroys sin forever, disease and premature death are part of the curse placed on humanity for Adam's sin.

It is only in modern times—when we have gained the knowledge and resources to better combat and prevent disease than ever before in history—that the existence of disease has prompted large numbers of people to question the reality of God. In a perverse twist of fallen human nature, the better we have it, the more we seem to question the loving character of our Creator!

Be that as it may, I'd like to suggest four responses to the question "Where was God when this disease attacked?"

1. Untimely death and debilitating disease can strike anyone.

In a fallen world like ours, illness and disease can strike down anyone at any time. While people who choose healthy, godly lifestyles are less likely to succumb to many afflictions (venereal disease, cirrhosis of the liver, lung cancer, etc.), there is no such thing as a lifestyle guaranteed to ward off all disease.

For example, one of the Old Testament's greatest heroes eventually died of an illness. After a faithful, fifty-five-year-long ministry that featured twice as many miraculous works as in the life of his mentor, Elijah, Elisha got sick—and died. The Bible simply says, "Now Elisha was suffering from the illness from which he died . . ." (2 Kings 13:14).

Keep in mind that this man, according to the Bible, was instrumental in restoring to life two people who had died (2 Kings 4:17–37; 13:20–21). Why did God allow this prophet—whom the Lord had miraculously used to heal others of their diseases (2 Kings 4:19,33–34; 5:1–14)—to die of a disease himself? It is a great mystery. And yet it should be noted that Elisha went to his deathbed with as much confidence in God as he showed throughout his long ministry (2 Kings 13:14–20).

This pattern continues to repeat itself in our sick little world, even today. People around the globe recognize the name of Billy Graham as one of history's great Christian evangelists. Millions have turned out for his crusades, and multiple millions more have watched him on television faithfully preach the message of forgiveness and peace with God through faith in Jesus Christ. Yet a few years ago it was revealed that Mr. Graham is suffering from Parkinson's disease, a chronic, progressive nervous disorder characterized by tremors, muscle weakness, and rigid facial expression. Neither a cause nor a cure is known for this disease, and the most that medical science can do is to help alleviate some symptoms.

Where was God when Mr. Graham was diagnosed with Parkinson's? The same place He had been since Mr. Graham accepted Christ into his heart so many years ago as a boy: walking alongside him every step of the way, even through the valley of the shadow of death. Mr. Graham preaches less these days because of his Parkinson's, but when he speaks, he continues to proclaim the same love of God for undeserving sinners that he has always preached. His physical condition has changed, but he knows that his God has not. As the apostle Paul would say, "Neither death nor life, neither angels nor demons, neither the present nor the future, nor any powers, neither height nor depth, nor anything else in all creation, will be able to separate us from the love of God that is in Christ Jesus our Lord" (Romans 8:38–39).

Disease and death are a part of the barren landscape on a fallen planet, but they needn't shake our confidence in a loving God. In fact, a big part of the reason Jesus Christ came to this earth was to free us from the ravages of disease. Matthew's Gospel tell us that Jesus healed the sick "to fulfill what was spoken through the prophet Isaiah: 'He took up our infirmities and carried our diseases' " (Matthew 8:17). His healing ministry was a foretaste of what He will usher in after His return, when "he will wipe away every tear from their eyes. There will be no more death or mourning or crying or pain, for the old order of things has passed away" (Revelation 21:4).

We're still living under "the old order of things," and that's why disease can still strike terror into our hearts. Illness and death are still very much a part of our world, and we look forward with great hope to that day, perhaps soon, when death itself will be destroyed (1 Corinthians 15:26). But that day is not yet.

2. All of us die—only the timing is unknown to us.

One thing about earthly life is certain for all of us: It comes to an end. Try as we might, we can't avoid it. Medical science has succeeded in lengthening life spans and improving our quality of life, but it cannot prevent death from winning in the end. It's a biblical certainty that "man is destined to die once, and after that to face judgment" (Hebrews 9:27). The only thing we don't know for certain is *when* our days will run out.

For some, those days slip away much sooner than anyone could have expected. That's what I learned as a boy in Argentina when my dad suddenly died of pneumonia. On that hot summer day I learned at least four things:

• *People die.*

Children don't normally think much about death. They may hear about it from time to time—Grandma died, Aunt Lily died—but on the whole they can't imagine what death really is. On the day my father passed away, I realized with a shock that people you know and love and count on actually die. They stop breathing, and you put their cold bodies in the ground.

• *Young people die.*

I realized that it's not just the elderly or the weak who die. My dad was a robust young man of thirty-four when he got sick and died. He was in the prime of life. Nobody expected him to die. But he did.

• *Dads die.*

When you're a kid, you think your dad is the strongest, most indestructible person on the planet. You can't imagine a disease strong enough to take your father's life. But nasty viruses and germs are out there, and one swept away my dad.

• *People become orphans and widows.*

When my dad died, I became the "man of the house"—at the age of ten. For the next several years I discovered how harsh life could be to a widow and her orphan children. I became well acquainted with both hunger and poverty, and never a day went by that I didn't miss my dad.

Had we known the date of my dad's death months or years before he left us, we could have better prepared for the dark days ahead. Yet none of us knows the time of our departure from this earth. We know we're going to die; we just don't know when.

One night on our television program I received a call from Mike, a twenty-seven-year-old man from Missouri. His dad was a retired Southern Baptist preacher, and Mike had grown up in the church. But at age thirteen he began to rebel, and church was now a distant memory.

"My life does not match up with the things I'm supposed to be doing," he told me. "I found out that there's a good chance I might have contracted AIDS. I'm addicted to alcohol, drugs, sex, and I just can't go on like this anymore."

Mike had taken some medical tests and was about to get the results. "I'm just real scared," he admitted.

"Are you willing to change, or do you want to drift along the way you are?" I asked.

"If I drift the way I am, I won't live much longer," he replied.

"This crisis is serious, and it's God's wake-up call," I agreed. "He's saying to you, 'Mike, My boy, you've been fooling around for fourteen years; it's about time you came back to Me.' "

Mike knew all about Jesus Christ and God and faith and forgiveness, but it took the likelihood of an early death for him to take God seriously.

Death does not come only to the elderly or the sickly. It comes to all of us, and often sooner than we expect.

3. We must always be ready to meet our God.

Although we are often taken by surprise when disease and death come knocking at our door, God never is. He has known from the beginning how long each of our lives would be. For that reason God is always prepared to meet us the instant we leave this earth.

The question is, are *we* ready to meet *Him?*

My father's death forced me to accept that death is coming to me and that I have to be prepared for it. In a significant way my dad's death made me the evangelist I am today. I realize that many of us are going to die younger than we suppose, and all of us are going to die eventually. Are we ready for it?

Thirty-five-year-old Bob called me a couple of years ago to ask for prayer. A year prior to his call he was diagnosed with AIDS. When he called, he was sobbing. I wanted to be sure he was prepared to meet his God, so I said to him, "We have all gone our own way. We've rebelled. We've been foolish. We've sinned against the Lord. But that's what the cross is all about.

"Jesus loves you wildly, Bob. He went to a cross for you. He loves homosexuals. He loves heterosexuals. He loves you with a passion, and He wants to give you eternal life and the assurance of it. Your body is infected with HIV because of lifestyle decisions you have made, but the body will be buried. Your soul and your spirit can go straight into the presence of the Lord, and one day when your body is resurrected it'll be a new body, never again to be infected, never again to suffer pain or tears."

That night I had the privilege of leading Bob to a vital faith in the Lord Jesus Christ, and he gained the assurance that he was fully ready to meet his God. He began to learn the wisdom of David's ancient prayer: "One thing I ask of the LORD, this is what I seek: that I may dwell in the house of the LORD all the days of my life, to gaze upon the beauty of the LORD and to seek him in his temple" (Psalm 27:4).

The reality of heaven gives perspective on serious illness. Sickness will not last, but heaven is eternal. Unfortunately, modern Christians tend to downplay the Bible's emphasis on heaven. Heaven is not a doctrine only for the aged or for those who don't have long to live. And it isn't a fictional teaching designed to take the minds of suffering people off their woes, as if it were some sort of theological placebo.

Heaven is a real place being prepared even now for those who put their faith in Jesus Christ. Jesus Himself promised His disciples, "In my Father's house are many rooms; if it were not so, I would have told you. I am going there to prepare a place for you. And if I go and prepare a place for you, I will come back and take you to be with me that you also may be where I am" (John 14:2–3). Heaven is not an escapist doctrine; in fact, heaven—not earth—is the ultimate reality.

So think much about heaven and study what the Bible says about it. The Scripture tells us far more about heaven than most people realize. And although it sometimes uses figurative language to describe our eternal home, we need to remember that figurative language is used to convey a literal fact beyond our current understanding.

Heaven is a real place, it is wonderful and perfect, and even now it is being prepared for those who are ready for it.

Are you ready?

"But I don't know how to get ready, Luis," you may be saying.

The best way I know is simply to stop right now, where you are, and in the quietness of your heart talk to God.

I suggest that you pray the following prayer of commitment:

"Lord, I come before You humbly, in the midst of my heartache and sorrow. Yes, please forgive my sins. Thank You that Jesus died on the cross to cleanse my heart and rose again to give me new eternal life. Thank You that now I can enjoy the sure hope of heaven. Please heal me. And use me to share Your Good News with others. I love You, Lord, and will live for You all the days of my life. Amen."

If that's your prayer, congratulations.

You've made sure of heaven![1]

Then keep in mind that . . .

4. God may have several purposes for allowing a particular illness.

Intelligent people always try to understand, at least dimly, what purpose God might have in mind for the things He allows to happen. In my own experience I have seen Him use illness in several ways.

- *To lead some to Christ.*

Perhaps that's been your experience while reading this chapter. If so, again, let me say congratulations! It's the most important decision you'll ever make. When you think about it, compared to receiving eternal life, no other decision is nearly that important.

Sometimes it takes a life-threatening disease to wake us up to God. The psalmist wrote, "Before I was afflicted I went astray, but now I obey your word" (Psalm 119:67), and "It was good for me to be afflicted so that I might learn your decrees" (Psalm 119:71).

[1] If you've just committed your life to Jesus Christ, please write to me. I'll be glad to correspond with you and send you a free copy of my book, *Your New Life with Christ*. It's yours free for the asking. Or perhaps you would like prayer for healing. Again, please feel free to write. My address is Luis Palau, P.O. Box 1173, Portland, Oregon 97207, U.S.A. E-mail: palau@palau.org.

God often uses disease and illness to awaken people out of spiritual slumber and bring them to faith in Christ. Many of us are so stubborn that we will not think of God or eternity until we must plan our own funerals.

In the Old Testament God said about His rebellious people, "Perhaps when the people of Judah hear about every disaster I plan to inflict on them, each of them will turn from his wicked way; then I will forgive their wickedness and their sin" (Jeremiah 36:3). You see, pain and disease are not the worst fate that can overtake us. An eternity separated from God is far worse—and God has done everything necessary to make sure that none of us has to suffer it. That is what I told Larry the night he called to confess his fears about his battle with AIDS.

When Larry called, my show's producers told me I had only twelve minutes of air time left. I thought, *Twelve minutes? I have to lead him to Christ. I have to lead this guy to eternal life.* I was praying that he would be honest, and I said, "Larry, it's your lifestyle that brought it on you, am I right?"

"Yes," he admitted. He had no desire to argue.

"What you really want, Larry, is eternal life; isn't that why you called?" I asked. "You want to know if you're going to go to heaven."

"Yes," he said tearfully.

"Okay, that I can help you with," I continued. "Would you be willing for the Lord Jesus Christ to come into your life tonight, Larry?"

"Yes," he sniffled.

"Oh, I beg you to do it. Because even though in your failure and in obeying your instincts, you got into this, the Lord says to you, 'Larry, my son, I want you, I love you, I died for you. And I want to give you eternal life.' And Larry, eternal life is a gift of God."

I led Larry in a prayer confessing his sin and admitting his need of a Savior, and before we left the air he placed his faith in the crucified and risen Jesus Christ and received God's gift of forgiveness and peace.

"Oh, Larry, my dear friend, you have eternal life," I told him. "And even though your body is now falling apart because of AIDS, the Lord has embraced you tonight. He will uphold you. I believe He's heard our prayer, and I'm going to trust Him to take away the pain from you. But the beautiful thing, Larry, is that you and I will be with the Lord in heaven for millions of years. And then there'll be no more death, no more pain, no more sickness—thank God, no more AIDS forever—because we'll be with the Lord in His presence."

Four members of a San Antonio church followed up with Larry after our telephone conversation. These dear Christians took him to the doctor, got him to the hospital, and ministered the Word of God to him until he died six months later. My dialogue that night with Larry moved me so profoundly that even today when I watch the videotape, my eyes fill with tears.[2] The Bible tells us in Luke 15:7,10 that the angels in heaven rejoice whenever one person comes to faith in Christ, but I often can't stop crying.

It was very much like that when Michael called from Kansas City. This thirty-one-year-old gay man was HIV-positive, had lost his job, and was being evicted from his apartment. He called, he said, to find some guidance and "to find out where to go from here." I had him follow me in a heartfelt prayer.

"O Father in heaven," he prayed, "I have sinned against You and I am truly repentant tonight. Forgive me for hurting other men and for breaking Your moral law. Lord, I am a sinner, and I don't deserve Your mercy. But I fall on my knees, Lord Jesus, and I thank You for dying on the cross and for taking my sins and diseases on Your own body. Tonight, Lord Jesus, I open my heart to You. Please come in, Lord, give me eternal life and the assurance that I'll see You in heaven because, from tonight on, I am Your child. Christ lives in me!

"Lord, I love You with all of my heart. And however many days You give me, I want to speak well of Jesus and bring some of my friends to Christ. Lord Jesus, help me with my housing now, and with my income. Give me some friends, Lord, who will not take advantage of me but be a blessing to my life. I pray this, O Lord, with great thanksgiving, because You're my Savior and my God. And I'll see You in heaven! In Christ's name, Amen."

I expect to see both Larry and Michael in heaven, and although I'm deeply sorry they didn't join God's family until they con-

---

[2] Anyone interested in receiving a copy of Larry's powerful conversion experience can contact us at the Luis Palau Evangelistic Association, P.O. Box 1173, Portland, Oregon 97207, U.S.A. Phone (503) 614–1500.

tracted AIDS, I praise God that He uses even frightful diseases to bring lost sons and daughters to Himself.

- *To lead others to Christ.*

In the great purposes of God sometimes it is His will to use one person's illness to lead someone else to Christ.

In Costa Rica one night I used Larry's story on the air, and nineteen homosexuals called in to give their lives to the Lord. In all, twenty-three gay men called the program that evening, and most of them were absolutely broken. I am not glad for the pain and suffering AIDS causes, but I am grateful that I serve a God who knows how to use even such dreadful diseases to prompt sinners like us to receive His amazing love.

In Chapter 1 I described my own wife's battle with cancer, a fight she nearly lost. Why would God allow my beloved Pat to suffer so terribly? Her pain must have had some meaning; as I said, an intelligent human being can't help but try to find meaning in the hard moments of life. I do know that when I have told Pat's story to audiences around the world, more than one stubborn, arrogant atheist has been shaken up enough to rethink his or her spiritual condition and surrender to Jesus Christ.

I think that's part of what the apostle Paul means in Colossians 1:24 when he writes, "I fill up in my flesh what is still lacking in regard to Christ's afflictions, for the sake of his body, which is the church." Our sufferings do not add anything to the substitutionary death of Christ, but they can be one reason that rebellious men and women come to faith in Jesus. In that way our sufferings can "fill up what is lacking in regard to Christ's afflictions." Some people will repent only when they hear of another person who has suffered undeserved pain and agony.

In Chapter 5 I told how the death of a young English girl named Mandy helped to bring her aunt and uncle to Christ. One of my fellow evangelists, Dan Owens, did a video interview with this couple in which he asked them, "What will you say to Mandy when you get to heaven?" Her aunt replied without hesitation, "I'm so sorry that you had to die young so that I would come to Christ." I don't believe God caused Mandy's fatal accident so that her aunt and uncle would accept Jesus' offer of salvation, but I do know that He delights in bringing great good out of deep tragedy. And sometimes He uses the death or illness of one person to bring someone else to Christ. That is part of His glory.

• *People listen carefully when suffering men or women speak.*

At a crusade service one night in Illinois the Reverend Kevin Krase told a silent audience how he had discovered a few weeks previously that he had terminal colon cancer. He said he told his doctor, "Don't tell me how long you think I'm going to live, because you don't know and I don't know; only God knows. I really don't want to second-guess God. He may give me more time than you thought, or less." He exhorted us that night, "Why do you have to wait until you have cancer to talk to anybody about the Lord? I'm guaranteed to be dead within weeks, so I have more clout. But you're going to die, too. So are the people you work with. We're all going to die, so just lay it out there. And if they get mad, it's their problem." He died a few weeks later.

Why are we so afraid that people will shun us if we tell the truth about heaven and hell? So what? Six billion others can be our friends.

People listen very carefully when a suffering person speaks. They respect the pain and sense that a suffering person has much to say that a healthy and comfortable person could never say. If you are suffering, you have a very strong platform from which you can honor God and share profound principles that a flighty, fun-oriented, lighthearted society needs to hear. Don't hesitate to speak when you have a chance to proclaim what you've learned through your pain. Speak up and share the lessons you've learned from God, lessons that only those who suffer can know. Those who suffer have experiences the rest of us know nothing about.

One of God's purposes in allowing your suffering may be to give you the privilege of comforting and instructing others. The apostle Paul wrote, "The God of all comfort . . . comforts us in all our troubles, so that we can comfort those in any trouble with the comfort we ourselves have received from God. . . . If we are distressed, it is for your comfort and salvation" (2 Corinthians 1:3,4,6). I admit that it seems an unusual way for God to comfort people, but it is His chosen way.

- *God may have purposes we can't see.*

I often meet people whose suffering makes no sense to me. I have no idea why they must endure such pain, but I am confident that God has a purpose in it that I can't yet see. I am sure that in heaven all will come clear and I will say, "Ah, now I see it!" The apostle Paul wrote, "Now we see but a poor reflection as in a mirror; then we shall see face to face. Now I know in part; then I shall know fully, even as I am fully known" (1 Corinthians 13:12). The "then" he's talking about refers to the time we will be with Jesus Christ in heaven. Many mysteries of life will have to wait until then to be cleared up.

My mother-in-law's paralysis, which I described in Chapter 1, fits in this category. I honestly don't understand why Elsie had to go through so many decades with a body crippled by polio transmitted through a tainted vaccine cube. She's far more godly than I am, yet she's been in a wheelchair since she was forty-five.

At one point she tried everything to be healed; despite her conservative Christian beliefs she would have visited a faith healer if she thought that would have brought a cure. We prayed for Elsie and did everything we did later with Pat, but the Lord said, "No, I'm not going to heal you." We don't know why, but when we get to heaven I think we'll find out. Only then will we be able to say, "I see the reason now."

God makes no mistakes, and He doesn't need to explain His purposes to us. And many times we must be content with that.

HOW DOES GOD HEAL?

I often pray for the sick in my crusades. I tell Pat's story and I read Psalm 103:2–3, which says, "Praise the LORD, O my soul, and forget not all his benefits—who forgives all your sins and heals all your diseases." I usually say that God deals with disease in one of four ways:

1. Every day of health we enjoy is a gift of God.
We should get up every morning and thank God that on this day we are healthy. Few of us have ever been seriously ill. Most of us live day after day, year after year, decade after decade, without

ever being really sick. We need to thank God every day for the miracle of strong, healthy bodies.

2. God sometimes heals by miracles.

I have seen and experienced miracles, instances in which people were healed in the most amazing ways. The Bible teaches that the Lord can and does heal through miracles, and I've seen them take place, especially in India and in certain parts of Mexico, Colombia, and Peru—poor areas of the world. I've seen people utterly and instantaneously healed. How? Not because I did anything, believe me. But because God is a loving God with power to heal.

3. God uses doctors, nurses, and medicine to heal.

God often heals by using the skills of health professionals and the techniques of modern medicine. We should remember that it was Jesus who said, "it is not the healthy who need a doctor, but the sick" (Luke 5:31). And yet it is not the doctors or nurses who heal, but God. As a surgeon friend of mine says, "I do the surgery, but God does the healing."

When my wife, Pat, came down with cancer, we did what the Bible instructs us to do in James 5:14–16. We asked the elders of our church to come to our house and lay hands on her. We prayed, we confessed our sins, they anointed her with a little oil and commended her to God. Then we sought out the best doctors we could find in the Pacific Northwest. They did surgery, she went through chemotherapy—and the Lord healed her. By the mercy and goodness of God, she's with me today.

4. Sometimes God chooses not to heal.

For reasons we don't understand, some people never get healed. We pray, we confess our sins, we anoint them with oil . . . and they eventually die. I have no answer for these cases. I don't know why God chooses to heal some and not others.

But I do know some things. I do know that God is a good and loving God and that He wants our best. I do know that He hears our prayers, even when it seems as if He doesn't. I do know that He is a God who can be trusted, a God who delights in doing what is right. And I do know that as God, He has an absolute right to choose for us whatever path He deems best. Sometimes we make so much of our human freedom to choose that we forget where that gift came from: God Himself. The Lord rightfully wields the ultimate power of choice, and there are times when we must simply accept His decisions and submit to His will, whether we understand it or not.

We must never forget that He is God, and we aren't. When we come to Him in faith and surrender our lives to Jesus Christ, He has promised to walk through all of life with us, both the good and the bad. And that is our greatest hope.

Every Inch of the Way

One night I took a call from Rosemary, a fifty-three-year-old mother of two grown sons. Doctors had operated to remove cancer from her lungs, then discovered that it had spread to her brain. By the time she called, she was having trouble remembering and walking and could not eat solid foods easily.

Even through the anxiety in her voice, however, I could tell that she was at peace. Both her husband and her sons knew the Lord, and she had walked with Him for many years.

So where was God when Rosemary learned she had cancer? "He's been there every inch of my life," she declared confidently.

Even the tough inches.

7

I JUST DON'T
LOVE YOU ANYMORE

Helen was forty years old, divorced, and despondent. Two men had walked into and then out of her life, and she couldn't see much of a future ahead for either herself or her ten-year-old son.

"I feel like Jesus doesn't love me or He doesn't care about me," she told me on "Night Talk." "I didn't really have a father growing up. I got married when I was twenty-one and was married for ten years, but he found another woman, took off, and that was it. I had a daughter with him, and he never came around to see us.

"Later I met another man. I had a son with him, but he never came around either. Now he's having a child with a woman he just married. He's going to be there, and I'm sitting here and watching all this stuff happen.

"And still I'm all by myself, even though Jesus knows I need somebody and want somebody. Yet I'm getting older, and it's not happening. I don't think He cares. There are people down here who aren't going to make it, and I just might be one of them."

Sadly, I receive many calls from women just like Helen. But don't think it's only women who struggle with the pain of losing a partner. I also speak with men like Frank, whose wife left him and his ten-year-old son three months prior to our conversation.

"I've heard that the Lord can heal physical ailments, but can the Lord heal marriages and relationships?" he asked me in a voice full of gloom.

And then there are the desperate calls from people like thirty-five-year-old Todd, still in agony after an unwanted divorce. After seven years of marriage his wife said good-bye because she said she couldn't handle his drinking. When she soon started dating her divorce lawyer, Todd said he "lost it," went to her place of employment armed with a knife, showed the weapon to her, and told her he was going to commit suicide.

Then Todd got into his car and rammed it into a tree at seventy miles an hour, breaking his hip and nose. Minutes before the collision he said he was "sitting by a lake, crying unbelievably. I was just looking to the sky and praying to God: 'I'm coming and I hope You accept me.' I don't know if you can get more sincere in your prayers than I was right then, just before I drove into the tree. But God wouldn't let me die."

DOES GOD DUCK OUT OF THE PICTURE?

The pain of any divorce can seem excruciating, but an unexpected or unwanted breakup can devastate those left behind. Often these hurting women and men feel bewildered, numb, even lost. What could have happened? How could their marriages have disintegrated so rapidly? And where was God when their wedding vows went up in flames?

Contrary to what some may believe, God doesn't duck out of the picture when an unfaithful spouse decides to alter the family portrait. God grieves with you when an unfaithful spouse says, "I just don't love you anymore," and He longs to bring comfort and healing to your broken heart. So where is God when your spouse walks out the door for the last time? Allow me to outline seven key principles for those devastated by unwelcome divorces.

1. Adultery is evil, and God hates it.
Although adultery either triggers a high percentage of divorces,

our society seems to have forgotten that having sex with someone other than a spouse is a terrible sin. The Bible could hardly be more emphatic about this. It says, "Marriage should be honored by all, and the marriage bed kept pure, for God will judge the adulterer and all the sexually immoral" (Hebrews 13:4). It also says, "Do not be deceived: Neither the sexually immoral nor idolaters nor adulterers . . . will inherit the kingdom of God" (1 Corinthians 6:9,10).

When someone gets involved sexually with a person other than his or her spouse, it's not an "affair" or "fooling around" or "meaningless fun." It's adultery, and it's evil. God says He hates it (see Malachi 2:16) and He has promised to judge everyone who engages in it.

Why does God hate adultery so much? Besides the wreckage it leaves in the form of ruined homes and scarred people, adultery cuts at the heart of what it means to be human. The Bible says we were made in the image of God. In other words, we reflect His character in many ways. For example, God is a holy God, and that means He tells the truth. Second, God is a loving God, and that means He delights in doing good to us. Because we are made in His image, we were designed to tell the truth and to love and do good to one another.

A big part of truthful loving is the making and keeping of promises. The Bible can almost be thought of as a collection of God's promises to us. Throughout the Bible God makes hundreds of promises to His children, and He is scrupulous to fulfill every promise He makes. Therefore, when we break a promise—especially one of the profound promises, such as "I will love you all of my life"—we are denying and even despising the God in whose image we are made. When we break that promise, we declare that we are unloving liars.

Divorce devastates so thoroughly because it means that a person has broken a sacred promise that his or her spouse took seriously. When a person is unfaithful, he or she violates a bedrock trust, a commitment designed to mirror the faithfulness of God Himself.

Perhaps this is why I find that a high percentage of women are so utterly shocked when they discover that their husbands have been unfaithful. They expect their husbands to be true to their vows, and when they discover that hasn't been the case, at first they refuse to believe the truth. My wife and I have seen this pattern many times—discovery, disbelief, denial. But when the reality finally hits home, the betrayed spouse is shattered.

We were made to trust one another, and when that trust is violated—especially a sacred trust like marriage—the resulting devastation is incomprehensible.

I believe that the ruin left by broken homes powerfully reveals the wickedness of the human heart. Almost nothing unmasks the wicked side of human nature like this—and no one escapes. Even sophisticated, educated, brilliant human beings are infected with this deadly moral virus. Not even those we elect to defend justice and uphold righteousness are exempt from the dark side of the unredeemed human soul.

This grim truth hit the front pages once more a few years ago when Sol Wachtler, former chief judge of the Court of Appeals of New York State, was arrested on five felony counts ranging from extortion to mailing threatening letters. For four and a half years Wachtler had carried on an "affair" with his wife's stepcousin, the thrice-married Joy Silverman. After breaking off the relationship, she began an affair with another married man, and Wachtler became obsessed with winning back her illicit affections. In a bizarre effort to disrupt the new relationship, Wachtler posed as a private investigator from Texas to harass Silverman on the phone (using a device to disguise his voice) and sent extortion letters threatening to expose the new affair. After the FBI arrested the judge, he pled guilty to a reduced charge and on September 9, 1993, was sentenced to fifteen months in a federal prison.[1]

We shake our heads and roll our eyes when we read stories like this, but we really shouldn't. The Bible says, "for *all* have sinned and fall short of the glory of God" (Romans 3:23). None of us escapes this "all," not the "highborn" or the "lowborn," not the Ph.D.s or the grade-school dropouts. Not all of us are adulterers, but all of us *are* sinners. And if we do not admit our predicament soon enough, often the result is carnage.

Dale called me one night from a hotel. He lived in Indiana and admitted that he had committed adultery—an "affair" his wife had

---

[1] This story is told in more detail by Linda Wolf, "Love and Obsession," *Vanity Fair*, August 1994, 42–56.

discovered. I have heard many such confessions from men, but it would be naïve to think that the gentler sex is guiltless. The other day I spoke with a man whose wife just said to him, "I'll see you, babe. You can keep the kids. I've got another man."

God sees all this and weeps. He hates both adultery and the devastation it causes. It is a terrible sin, and it will not go unpunished.

2. Don't blame God for other people's sins.

Occasionally I will hear someone ask, "Why didn't God stop my husband from sleeping with that tramp?" or "Why didn't God stop me from marrying that woman?" But in a world where God has given us the freedom to choose how we shall act, both questions are unfair. It is not God's fault that your spouse left you for some other lover. God has emphatically told us in His Word that adultery is evil, and He has given to us His Holy Spirit to enable us to live in a way that pleases Him.

In other words, no one can say, "I *had* to commit adultery." No one can say, "I didn't know it was wrong." No one can say, "God refused to give me the strength to resist falling into that person's bed." God cannot be blamed for the wicked choices of sinful people. The responsibility for sin belongs to the sinner alone.

Along that same line, the victims of divorce should not blame themselves for any mistakes they might have made in choosing their spouses. (Unless, of course, they chose a spouse in direct opposition to the guidance of God's Word, the Bible. For example, in 1 Corinthians 7 the Bible forbids Christians from marrying non-Christians. If a Christian marries an unbeliever anyway and the marriage later dissolves, he or she should have the honesty to admit that the decision to marry this person was itself a foolish and sinful choice.)

From time to time the victims of divorce wonder, *How could I have made such a mistake? Why didn't God stop me before I chose this person?* But we're part of a fallen race, and all of us run the risks of being alive on a fallen planet populated by fallen people. Sometimes you can make the wisest decisions possible and tragedy still results.

Still, I think God protects His people from most of the troubles that could overwhelm them. Until we get to heaven, we won't know how often God saved us from the disastrous choices we were about to make.

3. We must take responsibility for our own sin.

All of us are personally responsible for the sins we commit. Our sin is no one's fault but our own. If I commit adultery, I cannot blame my mother. I must simply humble myself and say, "I committed adultery because I liked this woman and I wanted to go to bed with her." But I cannot blame my wife or my parents or anybody else.

Some years ago a casual friend of mine, a successful professional, tried to explain away his adultery. It was pathetic. He said, "I could not stand it at home anymore. My wife wouldn't let me watch certain television programs because she thought they were bad." I said to him, "Bill, look. Tell me that you love these women. Tell me that you wanted to take them to bed. Tell me that you enjoy sex with flight attendants. Tell me anything like that and I'll accept it. I know human weakness. But don't blame your wife! I am not that stupid; I refuse to accept that lame excuse. It was your choice to commit adultery, not hers, so why don't you just admit it?"

It's amazing how often we try to shift the blame for our sins. Adam did it in the garden, and we've been following his wimpy example ever since. On a "Night Talk" program Laurie called to say that three months before, her husband of seven years had left her and their two boys, ages two and three. He had run into an old girlfriend and said he "couldn't help himself."

"There is no limit to the excuses people will make when they're trying to explain why they had a 'fling' and 'an affair,'" I said. "The rich say their riches drove them apart. The poor, that their lack of cash drove them apart. The famous say that fame was too much for them. They're all poor excuses. The fact is, adultery is born of the heart. People mention all their cultural conditioning and wild emotions because they don't know how to control their hearts. Adultery is destroying the United States of America. It's devastating. And the children never understand.

"I know the temptation is to ask, 'Why did the Lord allow it?' But the Lord isn't responsible. It's your husband who committed adultery, who left you, and he is to blame. He is responsible."

"But he tries to make me feel responsible for his leaving," Laurie replied tearfully.

"Don't let him do it," I declared. "Your husband is not only a faithless, treacherous adulterer, but on top of it, men often try to make the woman feel it's her fault. Either they're not kind enough or they're not tender enough or they don't know how to make love. They'll pull out any story. That is an old trick that comes from the devil himself. Don't let someone lay guilt on you for his adultery and faithlessness. You're not perfect, but that's no excuse for your husband to walk out with an old girlfriend and then lay it at your feet."

By the way, if *you* are the one who walked away, you should turn to God and say, "God, how could I be such a treacherous coward? How could I be such a treacherous person? Forgive me, God. Have mercy on me." Then you have a duty to call up your ex and say, "I am a traitor. I am an adulterer. I don't deserve your forgiveness. But please have mercy on me and forgive me."

Never try to shift blame! That's a trick for jellyfish, not for people with spines.

4. God can soothe the pain of abandonment and divorce.

Don't ever entertain the thought that God abandoned you at the same time your spouse did. God never walks out on us, although we often walk away from Him. If we will only reach out to Him through His Son Jesus Christ, He promises to stay with us, walk with us, care for us, and lead us into ever-greater experiences of His love.

The pain of abandonment and divorce is real and deep, but it need not be crippling or disfiguring. Pain does not have to be the end of this dark road; there is comfort and strength and forgiveness for all those who humbly accept the invitation of Jesus.

Perhaps the best illustration of this is found in John 4, where we are introduced to a woman who knew a lot about abandonment and divorce. Five times married and five times divorced, she finally gave up on marital bliss and decided instead just to live with a boyfriend. Jesus Christ went out of His way to meet her and to offer healing for her damaged emotions and withered spirit.

Jesus never excused her sin—instead He made her confront it head-on—but He did offer her forgiveness. She quickly recognized Him as the Savior of the world, put her trust in Him, and then ran home to tell as many of her neighbors as she could about the remarkable prophet she had just met. Intrigued by her reports, the townspeople came out to see for themselves what kind of man this Jesus was—and they, too, returned home with a new faith and eternal life.

This unnamed woman came to Jesus as a bitter, angry, confused stranger scarred by five ugly divorces, and left a woman of hope and vibrant enthusiasm. She not only found healing for her own ravaged soul, she helped bring healing and restoration to her whole community.

That is what Jesus Christ promises to do for all those who put their trust in Him. To those with parched souls He offers living water, and to those with hungry spirits He promises heavenly bread.

That is the message I delivered one night to Helen, the Maine woman I described at the beginning of this chapter. I encouraged her to place her faith in Christ and then to get involved with a solid group of Christians.

"You need to spend time with other believers to strengthen you," I told her. "I have walked with Christ for forty years, yet part of God's plan is that we meet together with other Christians. Not only do I go to church on Sunday, where I have a lot of friends, but also when home I meet every Wednesday morning with a group of eight other guys. These are sharp, educated, busy leaders, but we pray for each other. We encourage one another. We uphold one another. We call each other during the week.

Helen, you need to find a group in Maine with whom you can get together. Mature women. Happy women. Women who know Jesus Christ. Some may be married; some may be divorced like you. But they should all know Jesus Christ, and together you can strengthen one another. You pray for each other. You advise one another.

"Then dedicate yourself to teaching your little boy Bible verses. Pray with him every morning and every evening and before meals. Encourage him to find a good bunch of Christian kids and a good youth group from a strong, Bible-teaching church. You can guide your boy. You yourself can grow. That's the way; that's the future.

"And if God has a man in your life, He will bring him around. But you've got to be sure he's a committed Christian. You've had two men in your life already, and you have to be most careful that you don't step into a bad situation just out of frustration. You've got to say, 'Lord, at this stage in my life, I'm praying for a good man to come my way.' It's not going to be easy, but the Lord can, if He chooses, bring a select individual into your life. But first concentrate on growing spiritually and bringing your boy up in the things of the Lord."

Just as He did in the Gospel of John, Jesus today still brings hope and healing to people scarred by abandonment and divorce. Helen made this discovery, and so can you.

"But how, Luis?" you may be asking.

Why not stop right now, where you are, and in the quietness of your heart talk to God? You can place your trust in Him this very minute.

I suggest that you pray the following prayer of commitment:

"Lord, I come before You humbly, in the midst of my heartache and sorrow. Yes, please forgive my sins. Thank You that Jesus died on the cross to cleanse my heart and rose again to give me new eternal life. Thank You that now I can enjoy the sure hope of heaven. Please bring my ex-spouse back to You. Reconcile our hearts. Bring love, joy, and peace where there has been bitterness, sadness, and tears. I love You and will live for You all the days of my life. Amen."

If that's your prayer, congratulations.

Welcome to the family of God—who loves you with an everlasting love.[2]

Then discover how . . .

5. God can heal broken relationships.

Divorce is ugly and always leaves painful wounds, but Jesus Christ is an expert at bringing reconciliation to warring parties. Even when the marriage cannot be saved or restored, personal reconciliation can take place through the power of Jesus' cross.

---

[2] If you've just committed your life to Jesus Christ, please write to me. I'll be glad to correspond with you and send you a free copy of my book, *Your New Life with Christ*. It's yours free for the asking. Or perhaps you would like prayer for you and your ex-spouse. Again, please feel free to write. My address is Luis Palau, P.O. Box 1173, Portland, Oregon 97207, U.S.A. E-mail: palau@palau.org.

And heaven only knows how many bad marriages have been rescued through faith in Jesus Christ, the resurrected Son of God.

A few months ago a troubled couple in their thirties came to our crusade in Kansas City, Missouri. After the message that night the husband took his wife's hand and led her to the arena floor, where they both received Christ and where their shaky marriage received a new foundation. The wife, Jo Ellen, called our program that night to report the change that already was taking place in her marriage.

"Our marriage has been pretty rocky over the past year or so, and we've really strayed from our commitment to each other," she admitted. "We've lived with a lot of frustration and anger."

When she told me of the decision they had made that night, I got so excited I didn't want to let them off the phone. With joy overflowing in my heart I led her husband, Mark, in a prayer right over the telephone: "O God our Father, what a wonderful night this is. My wife and I are reconciled. But mostly, O God, we're reconciled with You. Bless our home, make us Your family. Bless our little girl and make us a light in the community. Bless my friends at work, that they will see a change in my life and some of them will come to Christ. Thank You, dear Father. I'm Yours forever! In Christ's name, Amen."

6. God can be your husband.

Sometimes intervening history makes impossible the restoration of a shattered marriage. But even in these cases God offers hope through faith in His Son. As the ancient prophet Isaiah wrote, "For your Maker is your husband—the LORD Almighty is his name— the Holy One of Israel is your Redeemer; he is called the God of all the earth. The LORD will call you back as if you were a wife deserted and distressed in spirit—a wife who married young, only to be rejected" (Isaiah 54:5–6).

These are not mere words, simple poetic phrases that sound wonderful but leave you empty. God means what He says, and He longs to bring you the joy and contentment that your failed marriage could never deliver. He loves you and will never reject you. He asks only that you give Him your heart, as broken as it may be.

7. *Reject bitterness by forgiving the one who hurt you.*

I know that divorce causes unbelievable pain and that this pain, left to itself, usually transforms itself into bitterness. I know also that this isn't true for rejected spouses alone; the children of divorce can feel the sting of bitterness just as strongly as adults.

Jared, an eleven-year-old fourth-grader from El Paso, Texas, phoned me during one of our broadcasts. His mom and dad were separated, and he called to tell me his father had taken away a pet donkey.

"How do you feel about that?" I asked Jared.

"Not so good," he replied.

"Do you have a hard time forgiving him?" I asked.

"Yes," he replied. "My dad left four years ago. I don't feel very good about him leaving my mom and me and my two brothers and sisters."

"It's very sad when a dad abandons his family," I said. "It's not only sad, you have a right to be mad. It's wrong for a dad to leave. It is called a sin in the Bible. It's one of the worst sins. God hates divorce. He doesn't hate divorced people, but he hates divorce because it hurts kids and it hurts the wife. Divorce is like a disease that hurts everybody. Your mom, I'm sure, cries a lot when she thinks about it. Your dad should be taking care of you instead of running off and leaving you.

"But you must forgive your dad, Jared. It'll do you a lot of good, and it will even do him some good."

But *how* does forgiving the one who caused the hurt benefit you? That is what I tried to explain to Sandy one night.

"I was calling tonight because I'm very, very depressed," Sandy told me. "I'm in the process of going through a divorce. I left my husband for a while, and I've had to come back for financial reasons. My husband had an ongoing relationship with another woman. I sleep downstairs, he sleeps upstairs. Monday I see the attorney. We're still working out the legalities of it. Our children are grown up and in college. I don't want to be mean to this man because he is a good man; he just has a weakness for other women. I was not unfaithful.

"It's very painful, and I'm scared. I need wisdom and guidance. I don't know how to deal with my feelings. I'm very bitter and I don't mean to be, but it's something that slides up inside of me and I feel terrible."

"Of course, when a man has been treacherous and has been unfaithful and broken his promises, respect for such a person goes down the tubes," I replied. "Not that any one of us is perfect, but it's one thing not to be perfect and another thing to commit adultery. He promised you love at the altar. He promised to be faithful to you. He is the father of your children—and then he just plain walks away from you. That is painful, and frankly, you have a right to be angry. There is proper anger, you know, but bitterness is another thing. And the Lord can pull the bitterness out of you from the roots."

"I need that," Sandy pleaded. "I need that because I don't want to be mean. The bitterness has made me a nasty person whom I do not like."

"Christ has more power than your bitterness," I reassured her. "What you need to do is invite Him into your heart. I can't do anything for you—but Jesus can. I want to bring the two of you together, and then I walk away. And He says to you, 'Sandy, I will never leave you. I'll never forsake you. I am with you always, even to the end of the world.' "

It's reassurance like this that broken people such as Sandy and another caller named Patricia so desperately need. Patricia was married for four years, with one child, but by the time she was twenty-four years old, her husband was long gone.

"My problem is that my husband cheated on me," she said. "I know I'm supposed to forgive, but it's been real hard for me."

"How did you find out that your husband had cheated on you?" I asked.

"I read a letter from the girl he was dating," she answered.

"Was it just one failure, or was it a consistent dating of this woman?"

"It was consistent, because she now has a little girl."

"How long ago did you leave?"

"Going on three years."

"So, right after you were married, he already started an affair?"

"Right."

"You're still hurting and crying, aren't you?"

"Right."

"I don't blame you. I have close friends and relatives who have been done in, just like you have. I think adultery is treachery. It is sin. It's breaking your word. It is breaking everything that God wanted in a man and a woman. You are right to be angry, and you are right to be sad. God hates divorce. God hates separation because it hurts people so much. God loves the person who's divorced, but He hates the action.

"God loves you, Patricia, and that is why you cannot go on this way. You're a young woman, and you have fifty years ahead of you. You can't go on looking back on a man who isn't worth your memories. You can't keep living in the past. The beauty about Jesus Christ is that He came into the world to deal with hurting people like you."

By that point in her life Patricia was ready to accept Christ's offer of eternal life, and after I led her to faith, I explained that she had some work ahead of her.

"Now, the next step is a big one—not an easy one—but it wasn't easy for Christ to die on the cross to forgive you and me," I said. "You still have the problem of your ex-husband. You will think about him often, but with the help of the Lord, you'll begin to think about him less and less.

"You must forgive him. It isn't easy. He doesn't deserve it. Say out loud, 'I've forgiven him. It's in the past. Like God in Christ forgave me, I've forgiven him.' Only then will you be free. Because until you forgive, you are tied with a chain to that guy who hurt you so badly, who treacherously dealt with you. Until you forgive, he's running your life every moment of every day. But when you forgive him, you can clear your conscience, you can clear your mind—and you'll be Patricia again, not the ex-wife of some crooked guy who did you in."

By forgiving the one who hurt you, you release yourself from the prison of hate. As one New Testament writer put it, "See to it that no one misses the grace of God and that no bitter root grows up to cause trouble and defile many" (Hebrews 12:15).

One of the best ways to prevent bitterness, I think, is to give yourself away in service to others. Don't allow your traumatic experience to eat you up; instead, allow God to redeem your pain as you empathize with others who are walking the same hard road you traveled. Divorced people who allow God to use their experiences for the healing of others are often the best and most sensitive counselors. They bring a strong note of humility to the human condition. And God can use them greatly.

HOPE WITHIN REACH

The world would be a lot better off if we entered marriage determined that divorce would never be part of our thinking (let alone action). The Bible may permit divorce, but divorce is never a good thing. It is surely nothing to celebrate, as certain leaders are advocating today.

Frank, the man I spoke about earlier, knows this all too well. And yet, when his wife left him, God did start bringing good out of the bad.

"At that point I tried to seek prayer and the Lord for really the first time in my life," he admitted to a nationwide television audience.

"I'm saddened but yet encouraged by your honesty in saying, 'I haven't given much thought to God until now,'" I replied. "I've been preaching for forty years around the world, and most of us don't seem to take God seriously until some crisis hits. The reason is that we are pretty stubborn. We believe we're self-sufficient and we think, *Oh, I can run my life. I don't need God. I don't need Jesus Christ.* Too late we realize that human nature is frail and that we ourselves are faulty and sinful. In your case, it took your spouse suddenly walking out on you.

"I met a twelve-year-old boy from another country whose mom left his dad, just like you, when he was eight. He came to talk to us at a stadium. When he sat down with a counselor, the counselor asked, 'What made you come?' He replied, 'I was at the park and somebody gave me a leaflet saying that Luis Palau was going to talk about how to have a happy home. I'm twelve years old, and my home is very unhappy. In fact, I hate women.'

"The counselor asked, 'Why do you hate women?' He answered, 'Because my mom walked out on us when I was eight and she left my daddy and me all by ourselves. When they said they were going to talk about a happy home, I wanted to hear. So I came, I heard, and even though I'm only twelve, I want to give my heart to Christ.' That boy received Christ twenty-two years ago, and today he is a great Christian leader—married, happy, with great children."

When I asked Frank if he was ready for his own personal encounter with Christ, he replied, "I would—but can the Lord help bring together my family?"

"He can and He will, as long as first you, and then your wife, both submit to Jesus Christ and both of you come together around the person of Christ," I answered. "But it's got to start with you, tonight, when you give to the Lord your sinfulness, your misbehavior, everything you've done that offends God and has brought you to this situation.

"I can't guarantee that your wife will come back or that she will be as honest as you are tonight and will say, 'Oh, I've messed things up. I've done wrong. Forgive me. I want to be reconciled with Frank.' If you receive Christ, He will give you extra grace and kindness and a forgiving spirit to speak with her and to try to bring her back to you—although it's first to Christ and then to you. The Lord might use you to bring your wife to Him and to yourself. But the first step is to put your faith in Jesus Christ. Then you will be at peace and then you can lead your son in the things of God. Your life will change through the intervention of God—I've seen it happen many times. Couples come together again.

"But I would urge you first to get your own life straightened out with God. Receive Christ. Let Him become your Lord and your master and God. Then you can begin to work toward your wife."

Frank was intrigued, but not convinced.

"I just heard of the power of God in my life, and I've had to seek Him out and to see how His presence can be felt in this situation," he replied. "I haven't seen anything in my little working so far. As powerful as they say He is, I just was hoping and praying that He could make Himself known in my situation."

Frank wasn't ready to commit his life to Jesus Christ that night, but he did want a booklet called *What Is a Real Christian?*[3] I hope

---

[3] Anyone interested in receiving a copy of this booklet can contact us at the Luis Palau Evangelistic Association, P.O. Box 1173, Portland, Oregon 97207, U.S.A. Phone: (503) 614–1500. It's yours free for the asking.

he read that little book and realized that the best hope for his broken marriage was to be found in Christ.

Jesus Christ has the tools to bring healing and new life to anyone who asks for His help—but that's the key. You have to ask. Otherwise the tools stay in the toolbox. And they don't perform many miracles locked up in there.

8

A Violation
Most Wicked

The call came during one of my speaking tours overseas. Indira, a twenty-year-old woman, had read one of my books and had some questions.

"Just a few weeks before you came," she said, "I took off with one employee at our office who is married, plus another girl and another married employee. We left for San Pedro Sula, pretending it was business—but we all knew we were going just to party and sleep together. But at some point I remembered your book and suddenly felt that what I was doing was wrong. So I left them."

Indira admitted that she had been having sex with several married men, but said she enjoyed it and she especially loved the closeness she felt with these men. I told her the men didn't really love her but wanted only sex. Maybe, she said, but still she was unwilling to end these illicit relationships. She just couldn't give up the attention and feelings of love she received from these men.

"These men do *not* love you," I repeated. "They only want to use your body for their pleasure. If you stay on this path, Indira, you may well end up a bitter forty-year-old woman with a ton of men in your past but no one in your present."

She quickly changed the subject. "I like to wear short skirts," she responded cockily.

"And what does your family say about your dressing in such a provocative manner?" I asked.

"I don't have a family," she replied, a little more humbly—and then she broke.

Between sobs, the whole sad story came pouring out. Her mother had not wanted her and had thrown her and her brothers out on the street when she was five years old. She was adopted by another family, but her four adoptive brothers sexually abused her for years. These repeated rapes pushed her into living by the philosophy *qué será, será,* and by her teen years she began dressing in alluring ways and dating married men. But her lifestyle was now taking its toll.

I wonder how many young women who were raped as girls end up like Indira. Many suffer in silence for years, never daring to tell anyone about the awful violation that continues to torment them many years later. Those who do speak out describe how their innocence was ripped away in an abominable act of physical violence, an act that changed their lives forever.

And many wonder, *Where was God when I was attacked?*

It's not an easy question to answer. For me the question becomes even more difficult when the victim is a little girl or boy. Such a crime is unspeakable, unthinkable, unimaginable. And yet it happens with sickening frequency.

I know personally several women (and one man) who were raped as youngsters. The wife of a close friend was raped repeatedly by her brothers when she was a girl. And a boy I knew in boarding school in Argentina—a weaker kid who couldn't defend himself—was repeatedly abused sexually by a few aggressive, older swine who preyed upon their frailer classmates. As far as I know, the school never found out about the incidents; at least, our teachers never did anything to stop them. The attacks sickened the rest of us, but no one ever dared talk about them.

Four Responses to Consider

Where is God when sexual violence is perpetrated on innocent victims? Why does He seem so silent? Why doesn't He inflict a heart attack on the attackers? Where is He when rapes occur?

This difficult question could take a whole book to answer, but let me suggest at least four things to keep in mind as we search for answers.

1. *The rape wasn't your fault.*

When someone is raped, only one person is at fault: the rapist. The victim should never be blamed for the attack. One hundred percent of the guilt belongs to the attacker, and none to the one attacked.

Sometimes victims look back on the incident and say things like "I could have dressed more modestly" or "I could have been more careful locking my bedroom door" or "I should have shouted" or even "Maybe in the bottom of my soul there was a little tinge of desire." But even if any or all of those things were true, the attack is still not your fault. You are not the guilty party. The rapist is. And you should not feel an iota of guilt for the attack.

Think of it this way: Would you feel such guilt if somebody beat you up and broke two of your teeth? Suppose some idiot punched you in the mouth when you didn't expect it. What fault did you have? Should you say, "I should have worn a mouth guard that day" or "Maybe in the bottom of my heart I really wanted to feel what it was like to have a mouth full of blood"? Of course not. Nobody thinks like that. And yet when it comes to rape, that is exactly how some people think. But it's invalid and wrong. The victim cannot be held responsible for being attacked. Total responsibility remains with the ones who choose to carry out the attack.

The word "choose" in my last sentence is crucial. In this world God allows us to choose how we will behave. He tells us what He expects, and He gives us the resources to act in moral and upright ways, but we have the power to choose hurtful and evil behavior if we so desire. Only rarely does God seem to say, "That's enough! I'm ending this behavior right now." (For a few examples of this, see Daniel 4:28–33, 5:1–30, and Acts 12:19–23.) He takes our freedom to choose seriously, and sometimes that means innocent people suffer at the hands of the wicked.

Don't think for a moment, however, that this scheme of things has escaped His notice or that His followers throughout history have been blind to tragedies like this. The Bible is unflinching when it observes human behavior, and it often records the most heinous sins of one person against another. A prime example is found in 2 Samuel 13:1–29.

That passage records the rape of a beautiful girl named Tamar by a young man named Amnon, a son of King David. Amnon laid a careful trap for Tamar, and when she realized his evil intentions, she cried out, "Don't, my brother! Don't force me. Such a thing should not be done in Israel. Don't do this wicked thing." Her desperate pleas fell on deaf ears, however, and the passage says, "He refused to listen to her, and since he was stronger than she, he raped her." That rape led to a murder, and the story degenerates from there.

Why didn't God step in and stop Amnon from raping Tamar? I don't know; the Bible is silent on this point. But Amnon had the God-given freedom to choose his actions, and he used that freedom to act in a violent and sinful way. Did Tamar share any of the guilt for her rape? Absolutely not. The Bible makes it crystal clear that Amnon, and Amnon alone, bore the guilt for his attack.

Rape is a violent act perpetrated by sinful people on undeserving victims, and those victims can be the most saintly people alive. Many years ago one of my personal heroes, Helen Roseveare, was serving as a missionary to what was then called the Belgian Congo. She had willingly and even gladly released her personal desires to follow a spiritual call. And yet one horrible day marauding troops entered the African village Helen served so faithfully and for several days gang-raped her, subjecting her to atrocities best left undescribed.

Where was God when *that* happened? Isn't that an ironclad reason for *not* believing in a loving God?

Not if you are to believe Helen herself. After recovering from her physical and emotional wounds, she returned to that area, loved the people, and showed no hatred for those who attacked her. I have heard Helen speak publicly about this grotesque incident and have come away amazed at her insight into human nature and her deep love for God. She understands more deeply than most that God sent His Son to die for *sinful* people, precisely to remake them into men and women who abhor sin and delight in honoring God. And she understands that her rape was not her fault.

2. You don't need to live in the past.

Rape so deeply wounds the human body and spirit that many secular health professionals give little hope to the victim that she or he can ever fully recover. They talk about scars that never disappear, wounds that never heal, and bleeding that never stops. Too often I have heard declarations like "This is so horrendous, you're going to need therapy for the rest of your days. Life will never again be what it once was for you. You must learn to cope, but you can never hope to fully recover from this hurt. It's simply too deep."

That may be true regarding therapies that bypass Jesus Christ, but it most certainly is *not* true biblically. The Bible insists that you don't have to live in bondage to your awful memories, even memories of a violent attack like rape. And I have seen with my own eyes many examples of real people who are living out this truth that the Scripture proclaims.

I know a woman whose uncle raped her when she was twelve. A year or so after the attack she was walking past a theater in a big city. She heard people singing inside and walked in to see what was going on. Someone was preaching on Hebrews 9:14 ("The blood of Christ, who through the Eternal Spirit offered himself unblemished to God, will cleanse our consciences from acts that lead to death, so that we may serve the living God!"), and although she had never heard the Bible or gone to church, she cried out to the Lord and asked for forgiveness for her own sins and for freedom from the emotional weight of her rape. "Lord," she said, "cleanse my conscience and memory so I don't have to think about it anymore!"

And He did. Today she tells me, "As soon as I prayed that prayer, it was as if it never happened. Suddenly it was gone." Of course, she didn't forget the attack; after all, she told us about it. But she said, "There was a clicking, a certain flipping of the switch, a turning of a key, and the memories were turned off. They no longer hounded me. They stopped coming at me like a movie that I couldn't stop or a video that I had to watch over and over again. They were just gone."

My wife and I consider this woman to be one of the most mature, godly, well-integrated, complete human beings we've ever met. She is *not* hounded by the memory of her attack and she is *not* shackled to her past without hope of release. And it was Jesus Christ who set her free.

Many people today think that "theology" doesn't matter, that it's a relic of a bygone and irrelevant era. What an enormously hurtful mistake! What human beings alone cannot accomplish, God can. When many secular health professionals say, "You're going to have to learn to live with this trauma for the rest of your life," Jesus Christ says, "Come to me, all you who are weary and burdened, and I will give you rest" (Matthew 11:28).

When I was a boy, I used to sit in the front row in church and listen to preachers say Christians were "crucified with Christ," "buried with Christ," "risen with Christ," "ascended with Christ," and "seated at the right hand with Christ." I never could figure out what they meant when they said believers were "identified with Christ." Today I still wonder about the profundities connected with this doctrine, but at least I have a better handle on how it can radically transform our lives in the here and now.

One day I was counseling a woman about a traumatic event in her life, and she kept repeating, "But I still remember it. I can't get rid of it. I can't get it out of my mind, and I don't know what to do."

"Leave it behind you," I told her. "When Christ was crucified, all your guilt was taken care of. Christ rescued you from the curse of the law, being made a curse for you. You were crucified with Christ. You died with Him.

"And this is the great thing: You were buried with Christ. That means you can leave everything behind. You can leave it behind and never touch it again. Then you are risen with Christ. All the memories, all the garbage, all the evil you've done and the evil others have done to you can be left right in the grave. So stop digging for corpses! Don't keep going back and bringing things up. That is foolish, hurtful, wrong, and it's insulting to Jesus Christ."

Corrie ten Boom, the late Dutch woman whose World War II experiences were so memorably chronicled in the film *The Hiding Place*, used to say, "God takes all our sin and guilt and throws them into the deepest part of the sea, and then puts up a sign that says, 'No fishing allowed.' " If you want to fish, go ahead, but it's foolish and you don't need to. And anyway, all you'll catch are decaying slabs of putrid flesh that'll kill whoever eats them.

You do not have to live with hurtful memories—if you allow Jesus Christ to take control of your life and are willing to trust Him and obey Him.

Some of you may say, "Oh, Luis, you just don't understand. You can never understand because you were never raped." That's true. I cannot understand the experience because I never had it. But I know what God says and I know what so many friends and acquaintances have said. Rape is a detestable crime—but Jesus Christ can free even victims of rape from bondage to their nightmarish memories.

After I spoke at a woman's luncheon a few years ago and told some stories of women who through the power of Christ were able to move beyond a hurtful past, someone took me aside and said, "You might want to use my story sometime."

This woman was sexually abused by one of her brothers. Yet today she's outgoing, attractive, a great mother, and an active church member. She's one of the happiest, most cheerful, most balanced individuals I've met. She had a tragic, horrible childhood. But while in college she committed her life to Jesus Christ. Immediately an incredible weight was lifted off her. She was able to forgive her brother, something only Christ can help us do. With the Lord's help she refuses to live in the past. Today this young woman is a vibrant person, a prime example of what Christ can do in the life of a person who trusts Him.

3. Rape doesn't have to spoil your enjoyment of sex with your spouse.
If you have truly experienced the forgiveness, burial, and resurrection of Christ, there is no reason that you should have to stay in bondage to painful memories. If your mind somehow begins to replay the old episode like an unwelcome video, quickly say, "Lord Jesus, take this away." And He will intervene. It is not necessary, wise, or right to replay the incident, so reject it. Concen-

trate on your spouse and enjoy yourself; take pleasure in giving him or her enjoyment.

Another friend of mine who was raped as a young woman has been married for many years. She and her husband have enjoyed a free, happy, and sexually satisfying life. Although they are very old-fashioned types, they often hint at what a good time they have—and we know they're talking about sex. The rape did not permanently harm her enjoyment of sexual intercourse. She is a living testament to the power of Christ to overcome even the trauma of rape.

That power can do the same thing for anyone. And not just for women; some studies have said recently that up to 25 percent of *boys* have been abused or mistreated sexually. Christ's power can work in their lives, too.

A short time ago my sister Matil, the family historian, met my former boarding-school classmate who had been raped. Matil knew nothing of what had happened all those years before, so she was puzzled when this old friend said to her, "Tell Luis that I've become a Christian, that I have three beautiful daughters and a wonderful wife. He will understand." When I saw Matil afterward, she said to me, "Your friend asked me to tell you this, but I don't know why. He said you'd understand."

I do. And if you allow the power of Christ to rule in your life, so will you.

4. Don't broadcast news of your assault too widely.

Most victims of rape don't need words of encouragement to be cautious about how and whether to tell others of the attack, but my advice is this: Only a few people need to know. Yes, certainly report the rape to the proper authorities. Yes, do what you can to ensure that others are not needlessly exposed to potential harm. But I don't believe that digging up sad and evil experiences helps anyone.

The world says, "Tell your whole story to anyone and everyone." I think indiscriminate sharing, however, can prove far more destructive than helpful. For good reason the Bible says, "For it is shameful even to mention what the disobedient do in secret" (Ephesians 5:12). Wisdom says to be very careful about how and to whom you tell your story.

I know a woman who as a young girl dated a boy from her

church. One day he said to her, "Let's go up to such-and-such a mountain resort and have coffee." She agreed, but when they arrived, it became obvious he had lied. The place was not a resort, but a cheap motel in an isolated location. And he raped her there.

She's in her fifties now, and we found out about the incident only a short time ago. I said to her, "I hope you haven't told too many people about this. It's so useless. Unhealthy curiosity is aroused." She made a mistake, probably, by telling her husband, which caused a lot of trouble. They stayed married, though, and have several kids who today work full-time in Christian ministry. But their marriage would have been spared much grief if she had been more cautious about telling the awful story.

In my view, few people need to know about what happened. Repeat the story only later in life if it seems redemptively appropriate as a counseling illustration for someone who has endured something similar. I have known of cases where a victim kept repeating, "Well, you don't understand." Finally these friends or counselors have said, "Oh, but I do understand. I was raped, and this is how I handled it. I know what Christ can do in these cases. What counseling often cannot do, what psychiatry often cannot do, Christ definitely can do."

If you can highlight the grace of God and the power of forgiveness and the blood of Christ and the new direction of life He gives, then speak—but cautiously. Rape is horrible, but it is not the end of the world. There is redemption in Christ. Jesus Christ can help you bury the ugly memories and leave them in the past.

I learned of the rape of one of our friends only when she gave us advice on how to counsel someone who had been abused. We had come from a background that insisted rape and abuse *was* the end of the world and that little hope for complete recovery could be offered. She said, "Look, this is what happened to me," and then told us her story. We were completely surprised, because we had known her for many years and knew nothing of it. That she had suffered any trauma in her past that could have caused a crippling emotional injury, even in the most minute way, was the last thing to cross our minds. She is the epitome of a mature, godly, peaceful, wonderful Christian woman.

Yet this woman didn't broadcast her story, but recounted it in brief only when by so doing she could help someone else. I think that is an excellent rule of thumb. As the Bible says, "Do not let any unwholesome talk come out of your mouths, but only what is helpful for building others up according to their needs, that it may benefit those who listen" (Ephesians 4:29).

A NEW NAME—AND A NEW LIFE

I need to tell you how my conversation with Indira turned out. In the course of our thirty-minute dialogue on live television, I told Indira that Christ loved her and that she could belong to Him and be part of His family. She began to cry and confess that no one loved her, but at least when she was with these married men of hers, she felt loved. I tried to declare tenderly that a man with real love would not have sexual relations with her without marriage and that her feelings of being loved would not turn these relationships into real love. I told her she was precious to God, genuinely loved, and that He wanted Indira to become His child.

"God has a plan for you, and you're not an accident, even if you're the result of a one-night stand," I told her. "It's still God's purpose that you're here. It's not the worst thing that could have happened; the worst thing is never to have been born and never to know what life is. You can find meaning and purpose and direction through Christ, Indira. You can leave the past behind. Ugly as they may be, the experiences you've had are as nothing when compared to what's coming up if you choose to walk with the Lord. You can really turn your life around and make it into something beautiful and redemptive."

I pleaded with Indira to let Jesus Christ into her heart, to cleanse her, to make her into a new person. And live on television, Indira tearfully prayed to receive Christ. I invited her to the stadium the following night for our crusade, and she came. A young woman standing next to her discovered that Indira lived near to her church, and she invited her to visit the Sunday service the next day. The pastor of that church quickly paired Indira with Lorena, a mature, single Christian lady, and the process of discipling began. They immediately sent Indira to a summer Bible camp, where she was strengthened in her faith. After returning from camp she joined a group of young women in Bible study and began to grow. Since then she has been baptized and left her job, where she felt constant pressure from the young married man with whom she had carried on an immoral relationship.

One of the first things Indira did after coming to faith in Christ was to stop wearing provocative clothing. She also changed her name, since her case had become so well known across the country. She enrolled at the local university to get a degree, and a couple of weeks ago I got a letter from her pastor. He wrote, "You remember Indira? She is now becoming one of the most faithful people in our church."

Rape is a horrible crime with tremendous and often long-lasting consequences, but even its devastating power is no match for the irresistible might of Jesus Christ. Indira and many of my friends are living testaments to His power, a power that He longs to exercise on your behalf. A power that is available to you now. A power that can break the chains of ugly memories and set you free to enjoy life as you never thought possible.

As the apostle Paul wrote, "The kingdom of God is not a matter of talk but of power" (1 Corinthians 4:20). And as Jesus Christ Himself said, "All power in Heaven and on earth has been given to me" (Matthew 28:18, Phillips).

It's yours if you want it. And it's only a prayer away.

"But what do you mean, Luis?" you may be asking.

The apostle Paul says, "Therefore, if anyone is in Christ, he [or she] is a new creation; the old has gone, the new has come!" (2 Corinthians 5:17).

Do you want to become a new creation in Christ? If so, why not stop right now, where you are, and in the quietness of your heart talk to God? You can place your trust in Him this very minute. The choice is yours.

You can talk to God using any words you wish, of course. I suggest that you pray the following prayer of commitment:

"Lord, I come before You humbly, in the midst of my heartache and sorrow. Yes, please forgive my sins. Thank You that Jesus died on the cross to cleanse my heart and rose again to give me new eternal life. Thank You that now I can enjoy the sure hope of heaven. Please heal

the scars in my life. Erase the painful memories. Make me a new person. I love You, Lord Jesus, and will live for You all the days of my life. Amen."

If that's your prayer, congratulations.

You're the newest member of the family of God![1]

---

[1] If you've just committed your life to Jesus Christ, please write to me. I'll be glad to correspond with you and send you a free copy of my book, *Your New Life with Christ*. It's yours free for the asking. Or perhaps you would like further counsel and prayer. Again, please feel free to write. My address is Luis Palau, P.O. Box 1173, Portland, Oregon 97207, U.S.A. E-mail: palau@palau.org.

9

THE FETUS IS GONE,
SO WHY DO I FEEL
THIS WAY?

From the moment she called "Night Talk," Kim was sobbing. A twenty-eight-year-old mother of four, Kim just couldn't take it anymore. Through hot tears she explained that she was in the process of divorcing an abusive husband who drank heavily. But as painful as that was, it really wasn't the reason she called. So why did she want to talk to me?

"I'm feeling a lot of guilt because I had an abortion," she admitted.

Through the years I have received a number of calls from women just like Kim. Women who found themselves pregnant, confused, and in desperate circumstances. Women who finally believed someone who assured them that an abortion was a safe, moral, quick way to solve at least one of their problems. Women who made their way to a health clinic where their baby's life was taken. And women who afterward felt a crushing guilt they could not explain or remove.

Inevitably these grieving women have a number of questions. If God really loves "all the children of the world," as an old song promises, then where was He when they agonized over what to do about an unplanned pregnancy? Is it possible for them ever to be forgiven? Why didn't He stop them from getting an abortion? Is He really a good God, as the Bible says? Or is He good only at creating crushing guilt?

MORE EVERY YEAR

Millions of women get abortions each year, and the worldwide numbers keep rising. Many see abortion as just one more means of birth control, a convenient way to keep from feeding another hungry mouth. A case study I heard illustrates this prevalent attitude.

A university professor looked out at his large classroom one day and said, "Let me tell you a story. Here's this poor woman who lived three hundred years ago. She's a peasant. She has six children whom she can barely keep fed and clothed. And then she discovers she's pregnant with a seventh child. If she were living today, what would you recommend to her?"

Almost as one his students raised their hands and said, "Abortion."

"Fine," the professor replied. "You just killed Johann Sebastian Bach."

By and large, our modern culture simply doesn't see abortion as a moral issue. And yet . . . it is a fact that although abortion is a far more common surgical procedure today than heart transplants or colon reconstructions, the latter never produce guilt-ridden patients while the former weighs down countless women (and many men) with unyielding regret, shame, and guilt.

Why? Is it because society approves of heart transplants and colon reconstructions, while it frowns on abortions? I don't think so—at least, not the society I live in. Our culture seems to bend over backward to call abortion a simple surgical procedure, the removal of a foreign object, the extraction of unwanted tissue. Abortion counselors strain to convince women that the "procedure" is not only morally defensible but morally right.

Yet these tormented women continue to call our television program. Just as Maria did.

"Last year I had this problem," Maria told me. "When I was pregnant with my second child, they hit me with a sixty-percent high-risk pregnancy, a sixty-percent chance of having a baby with severe symptoms—heart or kidney problems. I carried her to term anyway, and she was born very healthy. But three months later I got pregnant again, and I was very afraid of what the doctor had told me before. So I did something I never wanted to do: I had an abortion. Since then I haven't gone to church because I think I don't deserve to go to church anymore."

"Does anyone in your family know that you had the abortion?" I asked.

"Just my husband and myself," Maria replied.

"Did he support you in having the abortion?"

"Not at the beginning. We were having a lot of problems—money problems and marriage problems—so it was my decision. He didn't want to, but he told me it was okay if I wanted to."

Maria and I continued to talk, and eventually we addressed the topic of abortion itself. "Having an abortion is a serious thing," I said.

"Yes, I know," she replied.

"It's serious because it is taking a life that God put in your body," I continued.

"I know."

"Even though it is a serious sin against the Lord, God loves you. Do you believe that, Maria?"

"I guess I do, but . . ."

"You find it hard to accept?"

"Yes, because I know I was always against it and I don't know why I did it, but I did it. Sometimes I think I don't even deserve to pray to God. That He wouldn't even listen to my prayers."

"Maria, I'm glad you feel so seriously about it. Because it shows you have a sincere heart and that you really have the fear of God. Don't you?"

"Yes, I do."

"Maria, I want you to believe this. The apostle Paul says these words: 'While we were still sinners, Christ died for us' (Romans 5:8). Jesus Christ didn't die for 'Holy Joes.' He died for us sinners. It's sad to have had an abortion, but the Lord is a good God, and He loves you, Maria."

"But do you think He will ever forgive me for what I did?"

"He will forgive you. When Jesus was crucified, do you remember that there were two robbers on either side of Him?"

"Yes."

"Both of them made fun of Jesus Christ at first. But at some point that afternoon one of them repented. He was about to die within hours, within minutes, and he repented and said, 'Lord, remember me when You come into Your Kingdom.' And Jesus said to him, 'Truly, today you will be with me in paradise' (Luke 23:43). This man had sinned openly, yet because he was repentant, Jesus told him that in moments he would be in heaven. The Bible says, 'The blood of Christ will cleanse us from all sin' (Hebrews 9:14). Isn't that great?"

"Yes."

"First, when you come to Jesus Christ in faith, He declares you forgiven because of the cross. He says, 'Maria, I love you because I made you.' And then He says to you, 'Maria, you are so repentant and you feel so unworthy. I can forgive you.' Listen to what the Bible says in Hebrews 10: 'Your sins and evil deeds I will remember no more.' Would you believe that?"

"Yes."

"This isn't the word of Luis Palau, Maria. It is the Word of God. Would you like to give your heart to Jesus?"

"Yes."

"Can you believe that He will forgive you, thanks to the cross?"

"Yes."

"Let me give you another verse just to calm your conscience and so that you know how deeply Christ did the job on the cross. Saint Paul says some beautiful and shocking words: 'Christ has redeemed us from the curse' (Galatians 3:13). You feel you're cursed, don't you?"

"Yes."

"In a way you're right; all of us are. Yes, you had an abortion. I haven't had an abortion. My wife hasn't had an abortion. But we've done other sinful things. We're all under a curse. But then Paul goes on to say, 'Christ has redeemed us from the curse of the law by becoming a curse for us' (Galatians 3:13). So Christ died in your place on the cross to take away the guilt of your abortion. But there's more. The abortion is only one of your sins. You have other sins, don't you? We all do, Maria. But the Lord Jesus says, 'Maria, I died in your place. I took away your sin. I love you. You will never be cursed, because I was cursed in your place.' Isn't that beautiful?"

"Yes."

"That's what is called 'the substitutionary death of Christ.' That means that He was your substitute and mine on the cross. You were right when you said that you sinned and that you deserve to die for your sin. But Jesus says, 'No, no! I will die in Maria's place.' And He did. Can you rest in that, Maria?"

"Yes."

"Good. First, you have to invite the Lord Jesus into your life, Maria, and ask Him to come into your heart, forgive you, and give you peace."

"I have, but like I said, I don't think I deserve it."

"No, you're right. You don't deserve it."

"I don't. I know that."

"But Maria, I don't deserve it either. Yet when I was a teenager I gave my life to Christ. I don't deserve it. Believe me, I am sixty-four and I go around every day thanking Jesus that when I was a teenager, He came into my life. I would love for you to rest your conscience in the promise of God. We have peace with God through our Lord Jesus Christ. You need peace, don't you?"

"Yes, I do."

"The only way you can get it is by having Jesus in your heart. It's good to go to church, but you can't get it just by doing that. You have to receive Him. I will lead you in a prayer, and then let Him take over. Begin to study little by little what the Bible says, and you will be a new Maria. You will change, Maria."

"Yes, that's what I want."

"Your life will begin to change, and you will be free again. You will enjoy life, even more than before, because you will have the Spirit of God in your heart."

Maria is like so many women who continue to call "Night Talk" or who write to us for help,[1] eager to shed the gnawing guilt that plagues their every waking moment. In a moment of desperation these dear women made a choice they soon deeply regretted, and they do not know where to turn. They want forgiveness, they want peace, they want freedom—but they are profoundly fearful they will never know any of those good things again.

---

[1] Please feel free to write to the author at P.O. Box 1173, Portland, Oregon 97207, U.S.A. E-mail: palau@palau.org.

FROM BAD NEWS TO GOOD NEWS

The good news is that forgiveness and peace and freedom are all abundantly available to any of us who really want them, regardless of what we may have done and despite the overwhelming burden of guilt we may feel. But in order to fully understand and appreciate the good news, it is crucial first to come to grips with the bad news. So I think we must start there.

1. Abortion is a sin against God.

In the eyes of Western law, abortion is acceptable and even a "right"—but most of us know instinctively that it's pretty serious business. The sixth Commandment says, "You shall not murder" (Exodus 20:13). Killing an unborn baby is sin. Abortion is a profound offense against human life and the God who made life. Abortion is a heinous crime in the eyes of the Lord.

An abortion is unlike most other surgical procedures. It can't be compared to removing a cancerous tumor or taking out a ruptured appendix. Why? Because abortion is killing a human person. It is a terrible sin, and God hates it.

So why do women get abortions? Many are ignorant about the moral consequences. Some feel trapped by an unwanted pregnancy and don't believe there's any other way out. Others are desperately poor and can't see how they could feed yet another hungry stomach. Still others believe they've simply made a mistake and determine to get rid of the baby for what they consider practical reasons. They may think, *I don't want my body falling apart* or *I'm too busy with my career* or *I'm having too much fun to be tied down with a baby.* Another group believes that abortion is a way to continue to live a promiscuous, morally loose lifestyle.

Whatever the reasons for choosing an abortion, the act itself is both tragic and sinful. Elective abortion is wrong and morally indefensible.

I often ask myself why it is that the loss of a child—prematurely as we would gauge it—makes us so angry at the Creator and prompts us to question His existence, love, and power, yet we so freely take the life of an unborn child. Why are we so quick to denounce God for the sudden death of an infant and then approve the systematic slaughter of millions of babies through abortion? How can our anger know no bounds against a God who would allow a son or daughter to die of SIDS, yet we encourage women throughout the world to end unwanted pregnancies by dismembering their unborn babies?

We can do so because we are part of a human race that is in open rebellion against God.

2. All sexual immorality is a sin against God.

Before I get to the good news, allow me to make the bad news even worse. The real issue here isn't abortion; it's usually sexual immorality. The Bible says, "marriage should be honored by all, and the marriage bed kept pure, for God will judge the adulterer and all the sexually immoral" (Hebrews 13:4). It says also, "Do not be deceived: Neither the sexually immoral nor idolaters nor adulterers . . . will inherit the kingdom of God" (1 Corinthians 6:9, 10) and "Flee from sexual immorality. All other sins a man commits are outside his body, but he who sins sexually sins against his own body" (1 Corinthians 6:18).

Our society may insist that sexual activity between "consenting adults" is both acceptable and even normal, but God's standards do not shift with every change in the cultural current. God says that sexual activity outside the bounds of marriage between a man and a woman is evil. And He says that those who choose to flout His standards and break His rules will not enjoy eternal life or find a home in heaven. It's that serious.

I used the word "choose" very deliberately. God allows us to make our own moral choices; you and I are free to choose the course of action we desire. God does not coerce us into making those choices, nor does He usually prevent us from making foolish or wicked decisions. We are given the power to decide for ourselves what we will do in this or that situation. It is one of the greatest gifts God ever bestowed upon the human race. "Choose for yourselves this day whom you will serve" (Joshua 24:15), Joshua challenged the ancient Israelites, and that choice is still presented to us today.

That's why it isn't fair to blame God for preventing us from making poor or sinful choices. "Why didn't God stop me . . . ?" is an illegitimate question. He has given us the power to choose, and He doesn't take away that gift every time we are about to make a bad decision. We have no right to blame Him for our poor choices if our leading desire is to please ourselves. Jesus said that you can *"choose* to do God's will" (John 7:17). And Peter declares that "you have spent enough time in the past doing what pagans *choose* to do—living in debauchery, lust, drunkenness, orgies, carousing and detestable idolatry. . . . But they will have to give account to him who is ready to judge the living and the dead" (1 Peter 4:3,5).

Of course, God does not leave us drifting alone on a sea of difficult choices. If our primary goal is to please Him, He has promised many times that He will guide us in making the best possible choices. The psalmist made this very clear:

> *Show me your ways, O LORD, teach me your paths; guide me in your truth and teach me, for you are God my Savior, and my hope is in you all day long. . . . Good and upright is the LORD; therefore he instructs sinners in his ways. He guides the humble in what is right and teaches them his way. . . . Who, then, is the one who fears the LORD? He will instruct him in the way chosen for him. . . . The LORD confides in those who fear him; he makes his covenant known to them (Psalm 25:4–5,8–9,12,14).*

Jesus Himself put it like this: "Seek first the kingdom of God, and all these things will be added to you" (Matthew 6:33). This doesn't mean that hard choices will disappear, but it does mean that God wants to lead us in the way that is best for us. We can depend upon His Spirit for the strength to *do* what is best. But it all starts with our choice to align ourselves with God by placing our faith in Jesus Christ.

3. Jesus longs to forgive those who have had abortions.

Now at last we come to the good news! Although abortion is a horrible sin, Jesus Christ died on the cross to forgive those who have had abortions. No one has to live with the guilt of abortion. Jesus has provided a way out!

The ancient prophet Isaiah peered ahead through the centuries, saw the ministry of Jesus Christ, and wrote, "We all, like, sheep, have gone astray, each of us has turned to his own way; and the

LORD has laid on him [Jesus] the iniquity of us all" (Isaiah 53:6). He also wrote, "He [Jesus] was pierced for our transgressions, he was crushed for our iniquities; the punishment that brought us peace was upon him, and by his wounds we are healed" (Isaiah 53:5).

Hundreds of years later the apostle Paul looked back on the ministry of Jesus Christ and wrote, "God was reconciling the world to himself in Christ, not counting men's sins against them. . . . God made him [Jesus] who had no sin to be sin for us, so that in him we might become the righteousness of God" (2 Corinthians 5:19,21).

No one's hands are clean. Not mine, and not yours. That's why Jesus Christ left heaven to come to earth, lived a perfect life without sin, and then died on the cross to pay the penalty for your sins and mine. When He rose from the grave three days later, God was testifying to the world that His Son had the power and the authority to forgive the sins of anyone who would place their faith in Him. And when someone is forgiven by Jesus Christ, all his or her sin and guilt is paid for and taken away—even the sin of abortion. Christ paid the full penalty, and nothing is left to be cared for.

Remember Kim at the beginning of this chapter? This is the good news I was able to share with her. "When Jesus died two thousand years ago on a cross outside of Jerusalem," I told her, "He was thinking of you and He was thinking of the little baby that you had killed. He died for you, Kim, and Jesus said, 'I know Kim, and I'm dying for Kim back in Illinois.' He loves you, Kim. If you will ask Him to forgive you, He will forgive you."

I found that same forgiveness as a teenage boy growing up in Argentina. During our Chicago crusade a young journalist asked me in a radio interview, "How can you avoid being self-righteous as you stand there to talk about Jesus Christ?"

"I'll tell you how," I replied. "I can do that because I have a very low opinion of myself. I am unworthy. I am evil, and I'm a sinner. I didn't find the truth; the truth found me. I was going in the other direction, and one day God sent a young man who sat me down and nailed me down. He said, 'Luis, if you die tonight, do you know where you're going?' I said, 'Absolutely, yes'—and I knew it was hell. He asked, 'Is that where you want to go?' I said, 'No, I don't.' He said, 'Then why are you going there?' I said, 'I don't know.' He asked, 'Do you want to change direction?' I said, 'Yes, I do.' He said, 'Do you want to do it now?' 'Yes,' I replied, and he read me a little passage from the New Testament where the great apostle Paul writes, 'If you confess with your lips Jesus is Lord and you believe in your heart that God raised him from the dead, you shall be saved.'

"He then asked me, 'Luis, do you believe in your heart that God raised Him from the dead?' I said, 'I do.' 'Then what else do you have to do?' he asked. I read the passage again and replied, 'Confess Him with my lips.' It was beginning to rain up in the hills of Argentina, and he put his arm around me and asked, 'Are you willing to confess with your lips that Jesus is Lord?' I said, 'Yes,' and he said, 'Okay, let's pray.' And we prayed.

"It was quick. It was in a hurry. He wanted to get back into the tent because it was raining, and I invited Jesus Christ into my heart. At that moment I received eternal life. And look at me now—so many years later—I know that I have eternal life because God forgave me that night in southern Argentina. He came into my heart. That's how I can avoid being self-righteous as I preach the Gospel."

Jesus longs to forgive you, just as He forgave Kim and just as He forgave me. Have you truly experienced His forgiveness? Do you know, based on God's promises and by believing in the crucifixion and resurrection of His Son, that your sins are forgiven?

The Bible says, "I tell you, now is the time of God's favor, now is the day of salvation" (2 Corinthians 6:2b). You can receive eternal life right now, just by placing your trust in Jesus Christ.

"But how, Luis?" you may be asking.

Why not stop right now, where you are, and in the quietness of your heart talk to God? You can talk to God using any words you wish, of course.

I suggest that you pray the following prayer of commitment:

"Lord, I come before You humbly, in the midst of my heartache and sorrow. Yes, please forgive my sins, including the sin of abortion. Thank You that Jesus died on the cross to cleanse my heart and rose again to give me new eternal life. Thank You that now I can enjoy the sure hope of heaven. I love You, Lord, and will live for You all the days of my life. Amen."

If that's your prayer, congratulations.

Welcome to the family of God!²
You can now discover for yourself that . . .

4. The Lord Jesus Christ wants us to enjoy deep peace.

One of the best things about being a Christian is the deep peace
that God brings to our heart. Not only does He forgive us, but He
gives us a new heart—a clean heart, free of guilt and shame and a
troubled conscience.

When I talk to women struggling with guilt over an abortion, I
love to quote Hebrews 9:14, a verse from the New Testament that
gives an amazing promise. It says, "The blood of Christ, who
through the eternal Spirit offered himself unblemished to God,
[will] cleanse our consciences from acts that lead to death, so that
we may serve the living God!"

I quoted this verse to Kim and told her, "Jesus will cleanse your
conscience from all these sad memories, and in the eyes of God
you will be as pure and clean as when you were a five-year-old
little girl, without a stain in the eyes of God." And she believed
God's promise!

A New Testament scholar, C. H. Dodd, once said that the word
translated as "cleanse" can actually be rendered "disinfect," so
that the verse could read "the blood of Christ will *disinfect* us from
all sin." What a tremendous thought!

When you are forgiven by faith through the blood of Christ, you
are cleansed and disinfected from *all* sin. You must come to rest in
the finished work of Christ, in His crucifixion, burial, and resurrection. Your sins and guilt have been nailed to the cross and buried
with Christ in the grave. You must leave them behind.

Many people struggle with this. They can believe that God will
forgive them when they put their trust in Christ, but they allow
their forgiven sins to haunt them still. This was exactly the problem for one woman who sought out Christian author Rebecca
Manley Pippert. Becky told the following story several years
ago:

² If you've just committed your life to Jesus Christ, please write to me. I'll be glad
to correspond with you and send you a free copy of my book, *Your New Life with
Christ*. It's yours free for the asking. Or perhaps you would like further counsel
and prayer. Again, please feel free to write. My address is Luis Palau, P.O. Box
1173, Portland, Oregon 97207, U.S.A. E-mail: palau@palau.org.

A few years ago a woman approached me at a conference I was addressing. She was lovely, godly . . . and utterly tortured. She kept sobbing and crying. She could hardly get out her story.

Finally, she began to tell me that many years ago she and her husband—who was then her fiancé—were youth leaders in a very conservative, evangelical church. They were to get married in July. But before the wedding came they began to have sex, and she became pregnant. The thought of what this would do to the church was more than she could handle. She knew her church just couldn't cope. But she said, "I also knew it was my own pride that I could not handle—here we were, counseling all these young people, and yet were not models ourselves." And so they never told anyone that they got an abortion.

"Becky," she said, "I believe with all of my heart that I have murdered an innocent life. We have had a wonderful marriage, been involved in ministry, and have four darling children. But I live every day with the guilt that I have killed life. I don't know how I ever could have killed an innocent baby. . . ."

As I listened to her sobbing and saw her torture, a thought came to me, but I said nothing. This could not be from God, I thought, it would destroy her.

She continued: "Becky, I cannot believe I ever could have killed an innocent one." This went on for some time. Finally I said, hoping this was from God, "I don't know why you are so surprised. Because this isn't your first murder. It's your second."

She looked at me, aghast, I continued.

"The cross shows all of us are crucifiers. Aborters or non-aborters, religious or irreligious. All of us show up as crucifiers when we look at the cross. We have all participated, killing the only innocent life there ever was. Our sins are precisely what drove Him there. And yet you seem more surprised that you can kill your own child, when you have already killed God's Child."

She stopped crying and looked at me. "That's true," she said. "You're right. I have, in fact, felt more guilty over killing my own son than in killing God's. You're saying that I have done something even worse than what I am confessing. Before, I couldn't imagine anything worse than what I did. But you are telling me that the cross shows me I'm even worse than I thought."

She continued, "Becky, if the cross reveals to me that I am even

worse than what I thought, it also reveals that the worst thing
anyone could ever do has been forgiven. Becky, the cross shows me
that the worst evil in the world has been absorbed and forgiven.
And if that has been forgiven, how can my confession of this sin
not be forgiven?"

And then she looked at me, began to weep for joy and said,
"Oh Becky, talk about amazing grace!"

Becky then addressed her audience directly and said, "I saw
someone walk right into the heart and mystery of the cross. I saw
someone literally transformed by a proper understanding of the
cross. It happened only when she took her sin and pain to the
cross, a cross that insists on highlighting our evil in order to leave
us absolutely no doubt that we have been forgiven.

"That woman intuitively recognized that God works according
to the deepest psychological law of acceptance, that for us to really
believe we are accepted we must know that we have been accepted at our most dreadful. That is precisely what the cross does,
and that is why we can face the darkness within, because God's
solution is so wonderful. That is what gives us the confidence to be
unafraid. We come to the cross and realize that there is no one who
will ever love us like Jesus."

Do you want peace? Do you want the confidence to be unafraid?
There really is no one who will ever love you like Jesus. He invites
you to come to Him and by faith receive His forgiveness and His
peace. I urge you to accept His invitation.

5. Tell others of God's mercy to you.

Once you have placed your faith in Jesus Christ and have been
forgiven and granted His peace, make a point of saying openly to
God and to people, "I owe so much to God. My sins that were
forgiven were so horrendous, I cannot repeat them."

When King David in the Old Testament finally admitted his
adultery with Bathsheba, he sat down and wrote the following
beautiful words to God: "Restore to me the joy of your salvation
and grant me a willing spirit, to sustain me. Then I will teach
transgressors your ways, and sinners will turn back to you. Save me
from bloodguilt, O God, the God who saves me, and my tongue
will sing of your righteousness. O Lord, open my lips, and my

mouth will declare your praise" (Psalm 51:12–15). Never forget what God has done for you, and always praise Him for His mercy.

Yet I would give one caution here: Use your experience most discreetly, and when you do tell your story, tell it with genuine, broken humility. You don't need to give details, and you don't have to keep harping on it. It was a horrible thing, and if you feel that you can tell your story to help someone else, emphasize that it was a terrible thing and that it was only by the mercy of God that you are forgiven and free from the memory and guilt of it. And then leave it at that.

Also, if you have (or will have) other children, cherish them. Be happy and grateful for the children God places in your care. With God's help, you can be a terrific mother. Show your children by your redeemed life that God loves them and wants them for His own.

6. You will see your little one in heaven.

Finally, let me tell you something that will jolt you and do you good: One day you will see your baby in the presence of God! Jesus said, "Let the little children come to me, and do not hinder them, for the kingdom of heaven belongs to such as these" (Matthew 19:14). That child of yours is in heaven, and if you have placed your faith in the crucified and risen Christ, you're headed for heaven, too. What a thrilling thought! It's the ultimate, unexpected, undeserved blessing. And it's exactly what I told Maria, the woman I wrote about earlier in this chapter.

"Now, you're a child of God," I told Maria after she accepted Christ. "When you die, you're going to go to heaven. Do you believe that?"

"Yes."

"In heaven you're going to see that little baby that you aborted. And you will know who it was, because that was a person. That baby is with Jesus, and you will see him or her. It won't be a baby, then, it'll be a full-grown human, and you will see that person for yourself. Isn't the Lord good? He not only forgives you, but one day you will see that little person. What a party it's going to be up there!"

A party I'm going to enjoy!

LASTING JOY

I can't end this chapter without returning once more to Kim, the mother of four who felt overwhelmed by her abortion. She called our program during Holy Week, with Good Friday just hours away. I was able to point her to Jesus Christ, and she gladly received God's mercy and forgiveness and peace.

Three days after our conversation I received some wonderful news from Kim's mother. "Thank you," she said excitedly, "I've never seen my daughter enjoy a day like the last twenty-four hours. She has so much peace now because she knows she was forgiven!"

That can be your experience, too. You, too, can enjoy twenty-four hours just like that—every day for the rest of your life. All it takes is accepting the marvelous offer Jesus holds out to you right now. Kim is glad she accepted it—and you will be, too.

10

PINK SLIPS
AND RED EYES

Y ou've climbed the corporate ladder, earned the lifestyle you always dreamed of, and cruised toward a comfortable retirement. But within five years of your expected farewell party, your supervisor hands you a pink slip—no apologies, no explanations. And suddenly your golden future crumbles to dust.

Scenes like that can play out even when a nation's economy churns along at high speed. Unemployment can hit suddenly, without warning. In just the past few weeks, while I've been writing this book, two more industrial behemoths have announced thousands of job cutbacks. Who would have thought such successful Fortune 500 companies would be forced to announce workforce reductions of such vast dimensions? Yet it's happening all the time.

Unexpected joblessness can strike anyone at any time. One friend had been a company executive for twenty-five years when he learned his services would no longer be required.

Another friend, the CEO of a major corporation, lost his job when he chose to lower company profits in order to save the jobs of seven thousand employees. His board of directors fired him for his efforts and took away the big pension he had expected to receive, forcing him to move to Northern California to manage a tiny company until he took an early retirement.

Few people know this man's real story. Ex-employees considered him a cruel and harsh man, but I know better. I prayed with him every week during those final days, and he often wept as he saw what was coming. I consider him a hero, like a man on the *Titanic* who gave his life to save someone else. Yet when he was fired, he was the one blamed for the seven thousand pink slips that immediately went out.

I often meet unemployed guys in their late forties or early fifties who despair over ever finding another job. Again and again they run into stone walls, either because they are considered too old or because their former salaries seem too high. These men say to prospective employers, "Don't worry that the salary seems too low; I'll take it." But they get turned down with a curt, "Yeah, you'll take it, but you'll be resentful when you realize you'll never make what you used to. You'll start thinking, *These guys are doing me in; they're not paying me what I deserve or what my experience demands.* No, we're sorry. You're not what we're looking for. But thanks for stopping by."

Other men and women lose their jobs when local economies shift from one dominant industry to another—or to nothing at all. We've seen this happen in Oregon in the lumber and aluminum industries. When a guy has worked in lumber since high school and suddenly there's no more work, he can't just switch to running computers. It's a desperate time.

Several years ago I was holding a series of meetings in Glasgow, Scotland, and the BBC challenged me about the local employment picture. "We have twenty-four percent unemployment here," they told me. "Probably a quarter of the people in your audience are unemployed. What do you say to them?"

"I never thought about it," I replied.

"Well, you'd better," they said, "because these people are desperate."

Their challenge forced me to consider what I would say to men and women driven to despair by unemployment. My mind went back several decades to my own experience after my father died. My mom, my sisters, and I all lived off my meager salary. But during one ninety-day strike I had no work. The unions didn't give us a penny, and those three months taught me a lot about unemployment and poverty. So what did we do? The following nine principles reflect not only what I did but what I now believe I should have done.

NINE PRINCIPLES FOR THE UNEMPLOYED

1. First, place your trust in God.

If you've already trusted God by placing your faith in the death and resurrection of Jesus Christ, great! If not, ask yourself, "What is God trying to do in my life in the midst of my unemployment? And how does He want me to respond?"

The Bible says, "Trust in the Lord with all your heart and lean not on your own understanding; in all your ways acknowledge him, and he will make your paths straight" (Proverbs 3:5–6).

So the first thing you must do is call out to God. In prayer, acknowledge your situation. It's actually more desperate than you think. The Bible says "all have sinned and fall short of the glory of God" (Romans 3:23). The Bible also says, "For the wages of sin is death. . . ." That's the bad news.

The good news is, "but the gift of God is eternal life in Christ Jesus our Lord" (Romans 6:23). Is Christ your Lord? If not, why not trust Him today?

"But how, Luis?" you may be thinking.

The apostle Peter tells us, "Salvation is found in no one else [except Jesus Christ], for there is no other name under heaven given to men by which we must be saved" (Acts 4:12).

Have you asked Jesus to save you? If not, why not stop right now, where you are, and in the quietness of your heart talk to God? You can place your trust in Him this very minute. The choice is yours.

You can talk to God using any words you wish, of course. I suggest that you pray the following prayer of commitment:

"Lord, I come before You humbly, in the midst of my heartache and sorrow. Yes, please forgive my sins. Thank You that Jesus died on the cross to cleanse my heart and rose again to give me new eternal life. Thank You

that now I can enjoy the sure hope of heaven. Please lead me to a new job where I can tell others about You. I love You, Lord, and will live for You all the days of my life. Amen."

If that's your prayer, congratulations!

There's no more important decision you'll ever make.

Then . . .

2. Don't blame others for your unemployment; take it as from God Himself.

A genuine follower of Jesus who is suddenly "downsized" or laid off or fired should take the incident as from God and not from a third party. When I spoke to the Glasgow audience several years ago, I urged listeners not to blame Margaret Thatcher or the government for their plight. "Forget the intermediaries," I said. "Third parties may be to blame, but for you to blame them is a futile, bitterness-producing mistake."

Instead I urged my out-of-work friends to consider their circumstances as from the hand of God Himself. Notice I didn't say, *"blame* God," but *"accept your circumstances* as if they came from God." There's a big difference.

We see this pattern repeatedly in the Psalms. Faithful men might be attacked by enemies or assaulted by the elements, but they consistently looked to God as the sovereign of the universe who allowed these hardships to come their way. "You made us retreat before the enemy, and our adversaries have plundered us," the psalmist cries. "You gave us up to be devoured like sheep and have scattered us among the nations. You sold your people for a pittance, gaining nothing from their sale. . . . All this happened to us, though we had not forgotten you or been false to your covenant" (Psalm 44:10–12,17). "You have shown your people desperate times; you have given us wine that makes us stagger," he writes (Psalm 60:3). "For you, O God, tested us; you refined us like silver," he declares (Psalm 66:10). "You have put me in the lowest pit, in the darkest depths," he says to God. "Your wrath lies heavily upon me; you have overwhelmed me with all your waves" (Psalm 88:6–7).

The Old Testament prophet Amos applies similar reasoning when he writes, "When disaster comes to a city, has not the LORD caused it?" (Amos 3:6). The pattern continues in the New Testament. "Endure hardship as discipline," the author of Hebrews urges us, for "God is treating you as sons. For what son is not disciplined by his father? If you are not disciplined (and everyone undergoes discipline), then you are illegitimate children and not true sons. . . . God disciplines us for our good, that we may share in his holiness" (Hebrews 12:7–8,10).

Don't waste time blaming intermediaries for your joblessness. Some superior may be at fault for your plight, but if you are a believer in Christ, nothing comes to you that doesn't first pass through God's hands. Whatever the hardship may be, consider it as His discipline to help you become more like Jesus Christ.

3. Try to find God's purpose for your joblessness.

"To search out a matter is the glory of kings," says Proverbs 25:2, and according to the New Testament, believers are both kings and priests. Therefore it is our "glory" to try to understand what God is doing in our lives. We all long for some rational explanation of our circumstances, and since we know that God is not irrational, we believe there must be some meaning in our life experiences. We want to understand them if we can.

I'm sure that one of the heroes of the Old Testament spent a lot of time "searching out" the reason behind the brutal hardships in his life. The story of Joseph takes up almost a third of the book of Genesis, indicating its great importance. Chapters 37 through 50 describe a dysfunctional family in which a deadly brew of jealousy, bitterness, and anger eventually bubbles over into betrayal and almost murder. Joseph's brothers sell him into slavery, and for several years one calamity after another befalls him. He is falsely accused of rape and unjustly thrown into prison, where he languishes for a long time.

Joseph must have thought, *God, what are You doing here? Why have You abandoned me? What are You up to?* To outside observers it had to appear that God had deserted Joseph, forgotten him, discarded him. Yet in his own time the Lord used Joseph's terrible circumstances for a great purpose. Joseph himself at last came to see this purpose, after God elevated him to great power in the land of his captivity. When his treacherous (and frightened) brothers returned to him years later, he told them, "You intended to harm me, but God intended it for good" (Genesis 50:20). The psalmist gives us further insight into God's purposes when he writes, "Then [God] sent someone to Egypt ahead of them, Joseph who was sold as a slave. There in prison, they bruised his feet with fetters and placed his neck in an iron collar. Until the time came to fulfill his word, the Lord tested Joseph's character" (Psalm 105:17–19, New Living Translation).

God may be doing many things in our lives by allowing us to lose a job. But one thing is for sure: As a father with his child, God is molding our character. So we ought to ask the question, "What part of my character most needs work?"

Those who serve the Lord Jesus Christ can rest assured that God will never waste their sorrows or allow them to suffer meaninglessly. I believe that a purpose lies behind everything that touches our lives, and our job is to find that purpose, if possible. If we're suddenly laid off, we can say, "I thought this was a great job, but God knows better. There must be a better thing for me to do than to work for this company. Now I have to find out what that is."

Remember my friend who lost his executive position after serving his company for twenty-five years? God had a better purpose for him, a fabulous ministry he never envisioned. When he lost his job, he thought, *I'll go to the Philippines like my brother and be a missionary*, but one visit made it clear that the missionary role wasn't for him. He found another job at a much lower salary, but still he felt restless. Then one day his church approached him about a staff position working with seniors. The church never considered approaching him while he held a "big-shot job," but now the time seemed right. It was! He felt he'd arrived in heaven as soon as the church opened the doors for him to minister to seniors. He'd never envisioned such an enjoyable career when at age fifty-three he left the business world.

Before I founded the Luis Palau Evangelistic Association many years ago, I also was fired from an executive position. Thank God, by that time I had learned these principles, and instantly I tried to put them into practice. For nearly three months I often sat in a rocking chair, trying to figure out, *Now, why did God allow this to happen? There must be a reason.* In the meantime I had to keep going, and we thrashed around trying to build our team from scratch. But I kept thinking, *God is dealing with me and my soul in the midst of this. He's trying to teach me something I wouldn't have learned any other way but this way. He wouldn't do this to me simply because He's on a kick. He wasn't looking the other way when this happened. I believe God has a purpose, and I need to find out what it is.*

The experience not only led to the creation of our team, it also made me realize that I had to walk more humbly with my God. It shook me up and demolished any pride in my abilities or winsomeness or capacity to charm people. God *did* have a purpose in what He allowed to happen—and He wanted me to discover that purpose.

4. Spend time alone with God.

Many of us claim we don't have time to pray—but unemployment changes all that. Suddenly we have all the time in the world.

If you are out of work, I recommend that you divide your days into distinct segments. In the first segment spend two hours alone with God on your knees. Read and study His Word, pray, and worship Him. Remember what the apostle Paul said about Scripture: "For everything that was written in the past was written to teach us, so that through endurance and the encouragement of the Scriptures we might have hope" (Romans 15:4).

Use this time to develop a heart for God, to nurture a sensitive, tender relationship with Him. Either suffering can embitter and turn you from God or it can bring you closer to God and better enable you to understand His mind and heart. So listen to God, go to excess if need be with the Bible, prayer, a notebook, and nothing else. Throw out all other books (even this one) and determine to spend time with God alone. Say to Him, "God, I believe that You have a purpose for me. Tell me what it is. What do I have to learn out of this? What are You trying to teach me? I am listening; the antenna is as out as it can be."

This is not a time to rail against God. Times of crisis should put us flat on our face and cause us to confess, "God, something's being taught here, and I am a willing listener. I am a humble slave. I want to learn everything I need to, because I don't want to go through this again." Rather than complain, argue, or rail, shut your mouth. As David said, "I will watch my ways and keep my tongue from sin; I will put a muzzle on my mouth" (Psalm 39:1).

As you spend time alone with God through His Word, keep an

open heart and let the Holy Spirit point out areas that need work or new directions He wants you to take. Above all, be open to the "new things" He may want to do in your life. Failure to do this can result in many long, miserable—and unnecessarily painful—years.

A man built a very comfortable lifestyle for himself and his family by working a profitable three-state sales territory. He owned several luxury automobiles and a private plane. Eventually he came to see the territory as his own property and began to get lax in his work. His wife kept reminding him, "You're getting careless, you're not following up on phone calls." But he ignored her.

Then one day the company was sold, and the man's new manager called him to the airport for a twenty-minute meeting between flights. "You're through," the boss told him unceremoniously. "No need to argue. You haven't fulfilled expectations, you haven't grown your territory, and your sales haven't gone up. You're done, and I've already given your job to someone else."

The man was so embittered by his firing and became so melancholy that his wife feared he might take his life. He refused to look for work and began to eat away at his reserves and investments. First the plane was sold, then a car. His wife took a low-paying job, and he eventually went to work as the administrator of a small organization. Still his bitter and angry spirit seeped through, and a cloud followed him wherever he went. Again he got sloppy in his work, and eventually this organization also fired him.

The second firing so embittered him that he dropped out of church and basically gave up on God and Christianity. Instead of learning a lesson, instead of humbling himself and saying, "God, what are You trying to teach me?" he got angry, and bitterness spewed out of his mouth. Former friends no longer wanted to speak with him; he wouldn't listen anyway.

This guy refused to discover and apply God's principles. In twenty years he learned nothing, and in fact went backward. He's a lesson in the negative and illustrates what can happen if we choose to be stubborn.

5. Volunteer at church or a service organization.
Spend four hours of your day volunteering with your church or a worthy service organization. Find out who needs help around the house or with their garden or a paint job or electrical repairs. Wid-

ows and the elderly can often use a helping hand; why not give them yours?

Cultivate a servant attitude and look for ways to help others. As the apostle Paul said, "Carry each other's burdens, and in this way you will fulfill the law of Christ" (Galatians 6:2), and, "Because of the service by which you have proved yourselves, men will praise God for the obedience that accompanies your confession of the gospel of Christ, and for your generosity in sharing with them and with everyone else" (2 Corinthians 9:13).

Don't stop working just because you're not being paid for it!

6. Join a team and evangelize your neighborhood.

Rather than sitting at home hoping a prospective employer will call, why not use some of your time to bring the Gospel to those who don't yet know Christ? Get a team together from your church and plan a strategy to evangelize your neighborhood. If it's summertime, put together a backyard Bible club and introduce the neighbor kids to the Lord. Your church can help you get the necessary materials. Or organize a neighborhood three-on-three basketball tournament. Or suggest a neighborhood block party. Use your time creatively to bring the Good News of Jesus Christ to men and women, boys and girls on your block who have yet to make a commitment of faith to Him.

Don't waste your time; use it creatively for the kingdom of God!

7. Start some new venture.

If you spend two hours on your knees with God and four more hours using a little elbow grease to help others, I recommend that you also spend another four hours a day looking for work or planning a new venture.

Do some honest self-evaluation. What retraining might you need? What are you good at? What do you enjoy? What unmet needs do you see around you? Whom can you talk to who might give you some creative ideas?

If I found myself out of a job, I'm pretty sure I'd get together two or three guys and say, "Let's start something new. What are our resources? What do people need? How can we meet that need?" And I'd just go. You can, too.

8. Plant something and grow it.

If you have a piece of land, however small, plant something, whether tomatoes or lettuce or potatoes or beans or whatever. And if you don't have a piece of land, borrow one. Many people would be willing to let you use a tract if you just explain your case. Say, "Look, I'm unemployed. I want to plant some vegetables. May I have a corner of your parcel?"

In Switzerland, the richest country in the world per capita, almost every piece of land not reserved for walking or the wild is cultivated. Everywhere you see little six-by-six plots where someone has planted something. Most of the Swiss don't need it—they have more money put away than anybody in the world—but if the rich can do it, why shouldn't the poor? Go find yourself an open plot and cultivate something. And in a little while you'll not only have something to eat, you'll also have the satisfaction that only farmers know.

9. Don't even think about bar-hopping or gambling or parties.

In Belfast, Ireland, many years ago I was visiting with a wife whose husband and son were unemployed. When the father showed up, I greeted him and we spoke for a short while. He complained about living off the dole and groused that the government stipend was too little for his family. Then he disappeared. He soon reappeared, all dressed up and looking great. "Bye-bye," he said.

"Where are you going?" I asked.

"I'm going to the races," he replied. What little he had he was going to waste at the horse track!

Many people do that. Instead of creatively investing their money, they blow it on gambling. Others go to the bar and sit there for hours, drowning their sorrows in alcohol and leaving even poorer than when they came in.

Unemployment is no fun, but you needn't make a difficult situation worse by wasting your limited resources on gambling, drinking, or carousing. Remember what the apostle Peter wrote: "You have spent enough time in the past doing what pagans choose to do—living in debauchery, lust, drunkenness, orgies, carousing and detestable idolatry. They think it strange that you do not plunge with them into the same flood of dissipation, and they heap abuse on you. But they will have to give account to Him who is ready to judge the living and the dead" (1 Peter 4:3–5).

We must all appear before the judgment seat of Christ, and He will be interested to see what we did with our time and resources. Use your time wisely during this season of unemployment so you can give Him a good report.

A GREAT EXAMPLE

Parade magazine profiled Herman Cain in its October 13, 1996, issue. An article titled "I *Chose* to Change My Life," explained how Cain rose from poverty to become chairman of the board of Godfather's Pizza.

But things weren't always rosy for Herman Cain. As a boy he slept with his brother on a fold-up cot in the kitchen of a three-room house in Atlanta, Georgia. His father never looked for a handout but worked three jobs to support his family: as a part-time chauffeur at Coca-Cola, as an evening-shift janitor at a bakery, and in between as a barber. Meanwhile, Herman's mother talked to him about God. "She taught me that success is not a function of what you start with materially but what you start with spiritually," Cain said.

Cain finished high school second in his class, then attended Morehouse College. He helped pay for his education by working after school and during the summer. He shined shoes, waxed cars, became a lab assistant at Coca-Cola, and clerked in a grocery store his father owned by then. After college graduation Cain worked as a civilian mathematician for the U.S. Navy. He then earned a master's degree in computer science from Purdue University and landed a job as an analyst at Coca-Cola. A few years later he followed a supervisor to Pillsbury, and at thirty-four became vice president for corporate systems and services. But after two years he grew bored and looked for another challenge.

What he did next illustrates many of the principles in this chapter. Cain realized that the only way to move up in the corporate world was to start at ground level, so he resigned his title, gave up his company car and nice new office, sacrificed stock options, and signed up for the operations-training track in Pillsbury's Burger King division. He learned the business from the bottom up, flipping burgers. "I did french fries," Cain said. "I cleaned the bathrooms. It was a humbling experience, but my own modest beginnings helped me to keep my ego in check."

Cain also knew that he was pursuing a solid direction because, "As with every major decision in his life, Cain turned to prayer for help. He got down on his knees: 'Lord, what do you want me to do?' When his wife noticed him lost in reflection and meditation, she told him, 'Don't worry—I know you can do this.' Cain accepted her words as a sign from God that he was making the right move."

Cain also knew that honest work is never "beneath" a man or woman, regardless of training or stature. He finished the two-year training program in nine months and was named vice president of the Philadelphia region, one of the worst-performing areas in the company. In four years he transformed it into the best region in growth, sales, and profits. In 1986 he was named president of troubled Godfather's Pizza, the company took off under his leadership, and two years later he and his vice president, Ronald Gartlan, led a team that purchased Godfather's from Pillsbury for $50 million.

"One of the keys to success in business is being happy with what you are doing, no matter what you earn," Cain declares. "Success is not the key to happiness. Happiness is the key to success. If you love what you are doing, you will be successful.

"And give God the glory. God is so good. Throughout my life, I've looked to God for guidance, but He doesn't speak through a letter or a telephone. Your spirit has to be open to His voice. He has often guided me through my wife, my mother, my children, my friends, experiences or a Sunday morning sermon."

You see, Herman Cain knows what it is to spend hours alone with God. He knows what it is to look for God's purpose in his life. He has dedicated himself to serving the needs of others and to giving God the glory for the good things in his life. He wasn't afraid to try a new venture, even though it meant an immediate (but not long-term) loss of income and stature. And I doubt very much whether he spent time in taverns or gambling casinos.

Allow Herman Cain to be a model. You might be poor now, but you don't have to stay in that condition. People might have abused or hurt you, but you don't have to allow their feet to remain on your neck. You might be out of a job, but if you're a believer in Christ, you're never out of opportunity. Partner with God, make a plan, work at it, and see what new vistas may open up for you.

What have you got to lose?[1]

---

[1] If you've just committed your life to Jesus Christ, please write to me. I'll be glad to correspond with you and send you a free copy of my book, *Your New Life with Christ.* It's yours free for the asking. Or perhaps you would like prayer about finding a new job. Again, please feel free to write. My address is Luis Palau, P.O. Box 1173, Portland, Oregon 97207, U.S.A. E-mail: palau@palau.org.

11

WHAT'S SO DIVINE
ABOUT ACTS OF GOD?

H ad you been planning for a summer wedding in 1816, you would have suffered a big disappointment. That year saw winter, then spring, then fall, then back to winter again.

The reason? In 1815 the Tambora Volcano on Sumbawa, Indonesia, erupted in perhaps the greatest explosion in recorded history. Before the eruption the mountain stood thirteen thousand feet high; afterward it stooped almost four thousand feet closer to the earth. The explosion killed fifty thousand islanders and destroyed the homes of thirty-five thousand more, while debris from the eruption darkened earth's skies for several months and caused a temporary global cooling that made 1816 "the year without a summer."

Of course, Tambora isn't the most famous volcanic eruption in history. With apologies to the Mount Saint Helens event of May 1980, that distinction probably goes to Krakatoa. In 1883 the island of Krakatoa, sitting in the straits between Java and Sumatra, blew its top. Its four-mile-wide caldera collapsed, causing a huge sea wave that reached 120 feet, taking thirty-six thousand lives when it smashed into Java and Sumatra. Krakatoa's explosions were heard twenty-two hundred miles away in Australia, and the eruption threw nearly five cubic miles of rock fragments into the air. Thick masses of floating pumice near the volcano halted all shipping. Ash spewed fifty miles high and spread over three hundred thousand square miles of territory, plunging the surrounding region into darkness for two and a half days.

This, friends, is what the insurance agencies call "an act of God."

Natural disasters come in many forms: volcanic eruptions, floods, fires, hurricanes and tornadoes, earthquakes. One of the worst earthquakes in history occurred in 1556 in Shaanxi Province, China. When the earth stopped shaking, eight hundred thousand people had died. A 1693 Sicilian earthquake killed a hundred thousand residents, while a 1737 quake in Calcutta, India, took three hundred thousand lives.

One question many people have when they read of (or live through) such unimaginable disasters is "Where was God . . . ?"

NOT A COMMON QUESTION

While I rarely get calls on "Night Talk with Luis Palau" from people who need to reconcile natural disasters with a loving God, the question must be raised in any event. Where was God in 1976 when a devastating earthquake took thousands of lives in Guatemala? Where was God when floodwaters ravaged America's midsection in 1997? Where is God when volcanoes erupt and obliterate entire cities, when wildfires incinerate whole neighborhoods, when hurricanes or tornadoes snuff out the lives of countless victims, or when blizzards cripple and kill stranded motorists on their way to church?

If God truly is "the God of all the earth," then why does He seem to be absent so often from its more turbulent hot spots?

I recently returned home from a visit to Argentina, which was suffering through some horrible flooding. When we approached Buenos Aires, our pilot flew the plane over my old hometown so I could see the place where I grew up.

But there wasn't much to see. Everything was underwater. As the pilot banked the plane around and headed toward the airport, he said, "There's the church; there's the market; there's this and that." He lived there himself and so knew the area well. In my day these were a bunch of small towns, but now the place is full of classy weekend homes. Yet their basements and lower floors were all underwater. It astonished me to see so many homes and buildings submerged, the dreams of so many people destroyed.

And it wasn't the first time I had seen a natural disaster up close and personal.

DISASTER IN GUATEMALA

In 1976 Guatemala suffered a violently destructive earthquake. I love the Guatemalans and wanted to get there immediately to see what we might be able to do to help. I had visited the country many times before for various crusades, we were frequently on Guatemalan television, and many thousands of its people had become my "spiritual children" by committing their lives to Jesus Christ through our ministry.

Immediately we sent two staff people, Jim Williams and Marcelino Ortiz, from our Mexico City office to Guatemala. I arrived about a day and a half later. Jim told me that one night he and Marcelino were staying in a downtown hotel when severe aftershocks hit. The pair grabbed their money and passports and at 4 A.M. ran out of the hotel in their underwear. Marcelino, a Mexican with a wonderful sense of humor, stood in the middle of the shattered road, looked up to heaven, and said, "Lord, if you're going to destroy these pagans, look! I'm a Mexican!"

Aftershocks continued to hit for several days. One night we slept in a school, but not very well. We shot up every time the earth started shaking. Finally we decided to sleep outside.

While there we learned that Billy Graham wanted to bring some immediate relief to the country. Some friends of his connected with large bread companies in Dallas were arranging to fly in a few planeloads of food. Billy himself was to fly in to assess the damage, and we set about to make the necessary arrangements.

We wanted him to speak to the President and the American ambassador, to pastors, to visit some of the devastated areas, and to give a brief message on national television. We tried for everything and got almost everything we wanted.

The whole communications infrastructure of the country had

been disabled, so making arrangements was difficult at best. Mr. Graham was flying in on a private jet from Acapulco, and we raced to the airport to meet him. What a bizarre scene. The airport was deserted—no immigration officials, no one stamping passports, no one even in the air-traffic-control tower. It was desolation, like a war.

Just before Mr. Graham's plane was about to land, we reached the airport, drove to a fence, jumped out of the car, and ran across the runway. Nobody was there to stop us. At one end of the airport we saw some activity and some soldiers, so we ran over there—and met the President of Guatemala. Despite our best efforts, we hadn't been able to locate him. And now here he was, in person.

"Oh, Mr. President, how are you?" I asked.

He recognized me from television and said, "Palau, welcome to our country! You've come to pray for us?"

After an emotional exchange of greetings he said, "What can I do for you?"

"Nothing, Mr. President," I replied. "We just came to try to help."

"Would you like to go with my son in a helicopter to see some of the worst damage to the country?" he then asked.

"Look, Mr. President," I answered, "we're here because Billy Graham is coming in just a few minutes. He wants to bring in some relief and do whatever he can to help."

"Oh, Billy Graham!" he exclaimed. "When I was studying at Fort Benning in Georgia, he came and spoke to the troops. I heard him. I respect Billy Graham. I even went to his crusade in Tulsa, Oklahoma."

"Well, he'll be coming in anytime," I repeated.

"Anything I can do for Billy Graham?" he asked.

How could the timing have been any more fantastic? Almost at that moment Mr. Graham's jet touched down, and the pilot found an undamaged spot and parked the plane. I ran over to the jet and was waiting when it rolled to a stop. When Mr. Graham got out, I said, "Hello! How are you? Here comes the President of the country to greet you."

Mr. Graham and his wife, Ruth, were standing in the middle of the runway when the President pulled up to welcome him.

"My son"—also named Luis—"will take you in a helicopter to see the damage," the President said. Immediately we boarded a Huey and flew over the devastated towns. At one point we landed in the middle of a town that, except for a few evangelical churches, had been flattened. Everyone made a big deal about that. In most towns the big churches were destroyed because they were made in the old days of brick and mortar, while the evangelical churches were made of iron and prefabricated materials that don't disintegrate as easily.

Everyone we met seemed to be in shock; dazed looks haunted all the faces. It was as if an atomic bomb had exploded. How devastating to see every house demolished and such subdued, almost catatonic expressions. We took a small tour of the village, prayed, talked to residents, took some pictures, then lifted off again.

Once we returned to the airport, we drove Mr. Graham into town and said, "Billy, we're going to meet with fifteen hundred pastors at a Presbyterian church downtown, and we'd like you to speak to them."

This building had been severely damaged in the quake, and even when we got there the ceiling was wobbling (it fell the next day). In the middle of Mr. Graham's message, another big aftershock hit. Half the audience got up, but Mr. Graham continued to shout his sermon while I interpreted. At the same time I looked everywhere for a way out in case the building collapsed. Soon the earth calmed down, however, so we finished and left.

In the car I said to Mr. Graham, "Billy, didn't you feel the aftershock?"

"No!" he replied. "When was it?"

"You were shouting," I said.

"I didn't notice," he repeated.

"But didn't you see half the audience get up and lift up their arms?" I asked.

"Yes," he said, "but I thought those were the Pentecostals just cheering about something!"

Next we took Mr. Graham to the only facility still functioning where we could videotape a TV spot for national broadcast. All the TV stations were down, but they thought they'd be up and running in a day or so. Outside a hotel, a news crew from ABC was waiting to get Mr. Graham's thoughts on the disaster; NBC and CBS showed up soon afterward, as did the BBC from London.

Billy thought we were geniuses: International news crews interview him, the President of the country greets him, he gets a helicopter tour of the disaster area, he speaks to fifteen hundred pastors. He didn't know that we had little to do with any of it. God is the only one who could orchestrate something like that!

I'll never forget that experience. When I first arrived at the airport—in a plane occupied only by myself and some relief supplies—everything was shut down. High windows throughout the terminal all were shattered; debris was scattered everywhere.

Several people recognized me from the frequent TV spots we used to run in Guatemala and asked, "Mr. Palau, do you think God is punishing us? Do you think Guatemala is more wicked than other nations? Is this why this is happening to us?" The President asked the same questions. What I told these hurting people then is still what I would say today.

WHY LET IT HAPPEN?

Where was God when the 1976 earthquake devastated Guatemala? Why did He allow it to happen? How could a good, loving God permit such a catastrophe? I think we can make several biblical responses.

1. We are part of a fallen world, and the curse affects all of us.

When Adam and Eve disobeyed God in the Garden of Eden and the Lord responded to their sin by declaring, "Cursed is the ground because of you" (Genesis 3:17), much more transpired than the introduction of a few weeds and thorns. It's not a minor thing when God Almighty curses something!

The Gospel of Mark provides us with a potent reminder of this. One day Jesus was hungry and looked for some figs on a tree in leaf, but when He found no fruit on it, He said to the tree, "May no one ever eat fruit from you again." The next morning the disciples found the tree withered from the roots up, and Peter remarked to Jesus, "Rabbi, look! The fig tree you cursed has withered!" (Mark 11:14,20–21).

But this was no surprise to Jesus. He knew what happens when God curses a thing; it dies. And our world *is* a dying world. Earthquakes are merely the death rattle of a cursed planet. Earthquakes and other natural disasters happen because we live in a world cursed by sin.

This means we ought to rejoice in every good day we receive, because in a fallen creation things could be far worse than they usually are.

2. God may choose to use natural disasters to punish specific nations.

In the Bible God sometimes uses natural disasters to warn and punish individual nations for their behavior. Not all "acts of God" are indiscriminate.

For example, it was through a natural disaster that God apparently destroyed the ancient cities of Sodom and Gomorrah. The Bible says "the LORD rained down burning sulfur on Sodom and Gomorrah" (Genesis 19:24), and modern explorations of the area show that it was rich in sulfur and pitch; perhaps an ancient eruption threw these materials into the sky, ignited them, and destroyed the cities just as described.

The Bible also describes a future incident in which armies invading Israel are destroyed:

> *Suddenly, in an instant, the LORD Almighty will come with thunder and earthquake and great noise, with windstorm and tempest and flames of a devouring fire. Then the hordes of all the nations that fight against Ariel [Israel], that attack her and her fortress and besiege her, will be as it is with a dream, with a vision in the night (Isaiah 29:5b–7).*

A similar event is pictured in the prophet Ezekiel:

> *In my zeal and fiery wrath I declare that at that time there shall be a great earthquake in the land of Israel. The fish of the sea, the birds of the air, the beasts of the field, every creature that moves along the ground, and all the people on the face of the earth will tremble at my presence. The mountains will be overturned, the cliffs will crumble and every wall will fall to the ground (Ezekiel 38:19–20).*

In these cases it is clear that God uses what we call natural disasters to punish individual nations. Yet it is a leap to claim that we can know today when similar disasters bear the marks of divine punishment. Unless God has revealed specifics in His Word, we cannot assume that a specific disaster is to be connected to a specific national sin. We simply don't know. Therefore, although the Bible does teach that in some cases God judges nations through natural disasters, without explicit biblical declaration we can never say whether this or that earthquake is divine punishment for this or that national sin.

In Guatemala's case, for example, I doubt whether that nation is any more sinful or wicked than many other nations. In fact, I think its record is better than that of a lot of other countries that haven't been hit by earthquakes.

3. Because we're stubborn, God must reveal His power in awesome, frightening, and sometimes destructive ways.

In September 1985, a devastating earthquake hit Mexico City, leaving thousands dead and thirty thousand Mexicans homeless. Our office in Mexico City was among the casualties. In fact, I wanted to use some correspondence we'd received from people who suffered through natural disasters, but all of our correspondence (up to 1985) on this issue was destroyed because of that quake. Letters we had received from earthquake survivors in Nicaragua and Guatemala, from victims of a tidal wave in Honduras, and from several other incidents were stored in the Mexico City office. But the quake so damaged the office, we decided that salvaging the correspondence was too risky. Our letters were all lost when the ruined building was razed. So all our natural-disaster correspondence was destroyed by yet another natural disaster!

The Mexico City quake rattled a lot of people, including the editors of a Marxist newspaper. This paper, officially representing the atheist philosophy, featured an unusual headline summing up the disaster. On the front page, in letters at least three inches high, it shouted, ¡O DIOS!—that is, OH, GOD!

This is simply amazing, that an earthquake would move a godless newspaper to scream out on its front page "Oh, God!" If the editors kept no thought of God in their heads, the *last* thought on their minds when a tragedy hits should be God. Yet it was the *first* thing that crossed their minds.

That, I think, is why God allows natural disasters to occur. We humans are so stubborn, a crisis is sometimes the only thing that will cause us to bend the knee and humble ourselves and cry out, "Oh, God!"

I'm not guessing about this. In the Gospel of Luke we are given what I think is the clearest teaching on this subject in all of Scripture. In Luke 13 Jesus comments on a natural disaster that took the lives of several "innocent bystanders." "Or those eighteen who died when the tower in Siloam fell on them," He said, "do you think they were more guilty than all the others living in Jerusalem? I tell you, no! But unless you repent, you too will all perish" (Luke 13:4–5).

Jesus never says that God caused this disaster, but He does allow the event to slap awake a spiritually slumbering audience. "These people didn't die because they were more evil than anyone else," Jesus seems to be saying. "This could just as easily have happened to any of you. None of you knows when such a disaster might overtake you. The question is, Are you ready? If your life were to end tonight in an earthquake, are you ready to meet God? If not, you need to repent and get ready!"

Jesus used the incident to remind His hearers that death isn't the worst horror to face, but rather dying without God. Natural disasters remind us of our mortality and our need to get right with the Lord. Notice how the psalmist makes this very point:

> As fire consumes the forest or a flame sets the mountains ablaze,
> so pursue them with your tempest and terrify them with
> your storm.
> Cover their faces with shame so that men will seek your name,
> O Lord
> (Psalm 82:14–16).

Natural disasters are horrifying. They leave destruction in their wake and broken hearts in their path. Yet they may also be one of God's most severe evangelistic tools. If we are so stubborn that we

will not consider God while life is good, perhaps we will cry out
"Oh, God!" when the walls fall in.

4. God rules over the world, come what may.

We must never forget that God rules over the world He created,
and that no earthquake or hurricane or flood or any other natural
disaster takes Him by surprise.

When I arrived in Guatemala after the 1976 earthquake, I
quoted Psalm 46:1–3 to the victims of the disaster:

> *God is our refuge and strength,*
> * an ever-present help in trouble.*
> *Therefore we will not fear,*
> * though the earth give way*
> * and the mountains fall into the heart of the sea,*
> *though its waters roar and foam*
> * and the mountains quake with their surging.*

And although I didn't quote it, it would have been just as appropriate to recite verse 8 from the same psalm: "Come and see the
works of the LORD, the desolations he has brought on the earth."
And I could have concluded with verse 10: "Be still, and know that
I am God; I will be exalted among the nations, I will be exalted in
the earth."

God often uses the power of nature to show His control of
planet Earth. With the prophet Elijah He used fire, an earthquake,
and a powerful wind that tore mountains and shattered rocks to
demonstrate His absolute rule and omnipotence (1 Kings 19:11,
12). In the Gospels He used an earthquake to announce both the
death and resurrection of Jesus Christ (Matthew 27:54, 28:2). In
the book of Acts He used an earthquake to open the heart of a
prison official to the gospel (Acts 16:26).

God rules, and even earthquakes and storms and fires can be
used to show His absolute control of the universe.

And one last thing: God also has the power to shield His people
from all the terrors of any natural disaster. As Isaiah 43:1–2 says:

> *Fear not, for I have redeemed you;*
> *I have summoned you by name;*
> * you are mine.*

> *When you pass through the waters,*
> *I will be with you;*
> *and when you pass through the rivers,*
> *they will not sweep over you.*
> *When you walk through the fire,*
> *you will not be burned;*
> *the flames will not set you ablaze.*

That is the kind of God I can serve with my whole heart!

AN AMAZING OBSERVATION

It seems strange, but when a natural disaster happens, few people tend to blame God. That's the amazing thing to me. People tend to blame God more in cases of man's inhumanity to man. I have been in many places that have suffered deadly floods or killer earthquakes. In Peru I found myself in the middle of one. But seldom have I heard people ask, "Why does God allow this?" Instead they seem to say to God, "Relieve us, protect us, take care of us!"

Why? My guess is that when you're about to die, if you don't get some help, you probably aren't going to ask "Why?" so much as "Where can I get help?" Later, sometimes, people ask these questions. But not often.

When they do ask the question, however, there's one answer that's always safe to give. That is, that although we are limited in our knowledge about "where God was when . . . ," we must say that the Bible has told us all we really need to know about life and eternity.

We'll never know *all* the answers, but we don't need to; we can trust and know the One who does know.

"But how can I know God, Luis?" you may be asking.

Jesus promises, "I tell you the truth, whoever hears my word and believes him [God the Father] who sent me has eternal life and will not be condemned; he has crossed over from death to life" (John 5:24).

Have you heard Jesus speaking to your heart? Do you want to receive His gift of eternal life? If so, why not stop right now, where you are, and in the quietness of your heart talk to the Lord? You can place your trust in Him this very minute.

The choice is yours.

I suggest that you pray the following prayer of commitment:

"Lord, I come before You humbly, in the midst of my heartache and sorrow. Yes, please forgive my sins. Thank You that Jesus died on the cross to cleanse my heart and rose again to give me new eternal life. Thank You that now I can enjoy the sure hope of heaven. I want to share this Good News with others. I love You, Lord, and will live for You all the days of my life. Amen."

If that's your prayer, congratulations.

Welcome to the family of God![1]

---

[1] If you've just committed your life to Jesus Christ, please write to me. I'll be glad to correspond with you and send you a free copy of my book, *Your New Life with Christ.* It's yours free for the asking. Or perhaps you still have questions. Again, please feel free to write. My address is Luis Palau, P.O. Box 1173, Portland, Oregon 97207, U.S.A. E-mail: palau@palau.org.

12

I'm Guilty,
Your Honor

R udyard Kipling said it well: "Nothing is ever settled until it is settled right."

Nothing seems more *un*settling, however, than considering the topic of making things right between God and ourselves, and ourselves and others.

Misconceptions abound concerning sin, guilt, and forgiveness. "Who believes in *sin* anymore?" "Why won't my guilt just go away?" We live in a society in which guilt and shame are now deemed illegitimate—but that does not eradicate either one. In fact, studies consistently show that about 80 percent of patients who seek out a psychiatrist's help do so because of unresolved guilt. Their problems are not caused by a congenital disease or a chemical imbalance or trauma to the head. Rather, a guilty conscience drives them to the psychiatrist's office.

I believe that guilt is also the reason many people turn their backs on God. Something they have done creates overpowering feelings of guilt in their psyche. As these feelings fester and grow, the guilt-ridden sufferers end up deeply resenting God. Despair eventually crowds out every other emotion, and they blame God for their feelings of utter wretchedness.

Of course, this isn't always the pattern. People don't always reject God so directly. Sometimes God simply gets left behind with everything else as a person's unresolved guilt chokes the very life out of its victim.

In one of his books author and psychiatrist William Glasser tells how he was called in to work with a mentally disturbed patient named Mary. The woman came from a well-to-do family, was married with children, and was highly educated and well respected in the community. At some point she began acting strangely, and despite conventional psychiatric help she continued to slide further and further into bizarre behavior. Finally the family had her committed to a mental institution.

Experts called her a lost cause and concluded that she had turned inward to hide from reality. Her speech gave way to grunts and other weird noises, and she stopped communicating with anyone. At that point Dr. Glasser entered the picture to see what effect his "reality therapy" might have on Mary. In reality therapy the patient is challenged to face reality, to take responsibility for wrong behavior, and to learn better ways to behave.

When Dr. Glasser first met Mary, he said to her, in effect, "Mary, I know what you're up to. I don't know what you have done, but I'm onto you. You have done something that so violates your conscience that you are covering up. You're afraid that if your husband or family or society finds out whatever it is you have done, they will think less of you. You're a decent woman, your reputation was good, you have a strong conscience—and this is your way of hiding. I want you to know, Mary, that you're not putting me off. And furthermore I want you to know that I think there's a way out. If you ever want to be out of this institution, if you don't want to spend the rest of your days in here, I can get you out any day as a sane person."

Throughout his speech Mary continued to grunt, makes noises, curl up in fetal position, and act in bizarre ways. Sometime later Dr. Glasser visited again. "Mary, do you remember what I told you the last time?" he asked (again, I'm paraphrasing). "I don't believe for a second that you're insane. I don't believe you're schizophrenic or mentally disturbed. You are a normal person, and this is your way of covering up something you did." Yet Mary showed no response.

On Dr. Glasser's third or fourth visit Mary greeted him at the door. "Help me out of here," she pleaded. Gone was her bizarre behavior, and she stood before Dr. Glasser absolutely sane. "If I'm going to help you out of here," he replied, "you have to tell me what you did."

"I've been a decent woman," she said. "My husband trusted me. My family thinks I'm great; we have decent kids and a good reputation. But I had an affair with my neighbor, and I can't face it. If this comes out, they're going to say that I'm dirty, that I'm a filthy woman, that I'm despicable."

"Well, now you have a choice to make," Dr. Glasser said. "You can stay in here for the rest of your days, or you can come out and admit what you did. And if they call you a bad woman and throw you out, that would be tough. But is it worse than this? On the other hand, maybe your husband will accept you, maybe he'll forgive you. If he doesn't, tough luck—but you can't stay here for the rest of your life."

Mary's is an extreme case, but not an unusual one. Guilt cripples a person's ability to enjoy life to the fullest. Left unresolved, guilt robs today of its strength and leaves tomorrow with nothing but sorrow.

THE PROBLEM OF FALSE GUILT

Not all guilt is created equal. While Mary's guilt was created by behavior the Bible condemns as sinful, some feelings of guilt arise despite the fact that no sin has been committed. We could call this latter guilt "false" guilt, feelings of guilt created in the absence of any moral wrongdoing. It may sound obvious that you're not guilty for that which does not bring guilt, but many people labor under mountains of false guilt.

In Chapter 2 I described the tragedy Greg and Linda suffered when their newborn daughter died of SIDS while sleeping next to them in their bed. Her death not only rocked Greg's world, it left him feeling intensely guilty for something not his fault.

"You should carry absolutely no guilt, Greg and Linda," I reassured this grieving couple. "No guilt whatsoever."

"But I *feel* guilt," Greg replied.

"Greg, but you mustn't," I said. "Just lay your burden at the feet of Jesus Christ. You need the peace of God, Greg. There is no reason to feel guilty. You know, Christ died on the cross for real guilt. We all have done plenty of things for which we are truly guilty; but you are not guilty for the death of your little girl. It just happened; that's the human condition. We're part of a fallen world, and these sad things happen. Years ago my wife came down with breast cancer and had a mastectomy. The Lord graciously healed her, but things like that happen in this fallen world. And so you must lay this burden of imaginary guilt at the feet of Christ, Greg."

False guilt is destructive and seems amazingly prevalent in this country. Of course, sometimes false guilt merely covers real guilt. More than once I have seen someone harp on some imaginary sin because he or she didn't want to deal with a real sin actually committed.

Also I think that sometimes we so strongly emphasize the damage of real sin that we make people feel guilty for things God forgave long ago. Sadly, I have done this myself.

Years ago I overpainted the picture regarding premarital sex. I used to say, "If you have premarital sex, you'll never know what real love could have been." My wife encouraged me to ease up, but I continued to repeat that statement until she finally said to me, "I am going to have to ask you never to say that in my presence again. That is entirely unbiblical. You've pushed it far out of reality. What's redemption all about? What's the love of God all about? And where did you get this? What makes you say such an outrageous thing?"

She then forced me to talk to a Christian woman I respected who as a teenager had been sexually active before her marriage and conversion—and I quickly realized how wrong I had been. I used to make that statement to emphasize the value of sexual purity, but an excessive truth borders on being a lie. The Christian community has overstressed the damage that sexual sin can do. If you had to pull out three rotten teeth, would that damage your humanity or make you less human? Does one bad eye diminish your dignity? Premarital sex is bad because of the real harm it causes and because God tells us it is, but we dare not go beyond what He says in His Word. We must carefully distinguish between real guilt and false guilt.

So how do we deal with false guilt? We must recognize it for the impostor it is. False guilt does not have to be confessed, repented of, or atoned for, any more than an imaginary goblin has to be hunted, trapped, and killed. You deal with both tormentors in the same way: You recognize that they are nothing but vapors and shadows, and you send them back to the land of make-believe where they belong. They have no existence other than the life we give them in our minds, and we can't afford to keep either of them breathing.

You're not guilty of that for which no guilt exists. Don't allow false guilt to plague you. God is the ultimate judge of sin, and if His Word doesn't condemn something as sin (either in particular or in principle), then it's nothing for which you should feel guilty. There is enough real guilt to go around without adding false guilt to the burden.

AM I BEING PUNISHED FOR SOMETHING I DID?

When tragedies overtake people, many instantly think, *Am I being punished for something I did?* Most cultures around the world accept some kind of tit-for-tat punishment and reward system. That is, if something good happens to me, I deserve it; if something bad happens to me, I deserve that, too.

A strong refrain of this idea can be heard in our own culture. One song in the film version of *The Sound of Music*—one of the most popular musicals in Western history—echoes this tit-for-tat philosophy exactly. When Julie Andrews's character, Maria, realizes that she has won the love of the heretofore unattainable Captain von Trapp she sings that sometime while growing up, "I must have done something good."

Many people feel innately that if something good happens, they somehow earned it; and if something bad happens, they somehow deserved that, too.

I wonder if this isn't one reason the Eastern doctrine of karma and reincarnation developed. It seems to explain the inexplicable. When tragedy strikes an apparently innocent victim, Hinduism sees the answer in an evil act committed by the person *in a past life*. After all, nothing comes from nothing; so if you get it in the neck, you must have deserved it. Even if your sin occurred in a previous life.

The Bible doesn't see things that way at all. While a few biblical cases describe some calamity as a punishment for sin, it sees most of the tragedies of life simply as a consequence of living in a fallen world. Otherwise, why would so many murderers and assassins live to a healthy, ripe old age, while so many saints die young, poor, and in pain? As the apostle Paul wrote, "The sins of some men are obvious, reaching the place of judgment ahead of them; the sins of others trail behind them" (1 Timothy 5:24).

When the psalmist tried to understand why evil people could prosper, he nearly lost his faith. He looked at "the arrogant" and "the wicked" and he said of them, "They have no struggles; their bodies are healthy and strong. They are free from the burdens common to man; they are not plagued by human ills. . . . This is what the wicked are like—always carefree, they increase in wealth" (Psalm 73:4–5,12). Such injustice made no sense to him, and he says he almost gave up his faith—until he saw the end of their story. "Surely you place them on slippery ground," he declared to God. "You cast them down to ruin. How completely are they destroyed, completely swept away by terrors! As a dream when one awakes, so when you arise, O Lord, you will despise them as fantasies" (Psalm 73:18–20).

It is usually inaccurate and fruitless to suppose that a tragedy overtook a person as a punishment for some sin committed in secret. The Bible rarely says that an illness or an accident is divine punishment for sin. Unless God tells us that some specific calamity is the result of sin, it is both arrogant and foolish to think we can discern the "real truth."

Therefore, when tragedy strikes, we should not leap to the conclusion that it is a divine punishment. It is possible that God is allowing us to suffer the consequences of our sinful decisions. But our hardships may simply be a consequence of living in a fallen world.

THREE WAYS TO DEAL WITH REAL GUILT

On the other hand, all of us do at times consciously choose to act in ways that dishonor and even insult God. That is, we sin. We violate God's standards. We choose our will over His. We ignore His commands and do as we please.

And that brings *real* guilt. When our guilt is real, we can't simply pretend that it doesn't exist. We may try to convince ourselves that it shouldn't exist, but there it sits and festers, impervious to our wishes. Real guilt is not like an imaginary goblin that can be banished with a thought back into nothingness. Real guilt is more like a dead fish lying on a white tablecloth in a hot, humid dining room. We can pretend that the fish doesn't exist, but our belief won't keep it from staining the tablecloth, smelling up the house, and making life unlivable for anyone two floors in either direction.

So how do we handle real guilt? Most of us try to deal with it in at least one of three major ways. And the first two don't work for long.

1. We can try to justify our sinful actions.
Have you ever noticed that dictators are always trying to explain why they butchered hundreds of people, or why their secret police had to kill thousands more? They seem compelled to make or find a law that justifies their brutality. They can't merely say, "We killed them because they were in our way" or "We killed them because they were a menace to our government." No. Instead they seem driven to give a "rational," "just" explanation for their actions. Guilt drives them to redefine evil so that under the new definition they can claim to be guiltless, even virtuous.

This is exactly what the Nazis tried to do in their war against the Jews. By redefining "humanity" to exclude the Jews and by passing laws to eradicate them, they attempted to portray their genocide as a heroic crusade. Yet the world disbelieved their vile ploy, and today the term "Nazi" is virtually synonymous with the word "evil."

We don't, however, have to look back to nations and World War

II for examples of how human beings try to justify their evil. We have only to look into our own hearts. We steal supplies from the office and tell ourselves that we're entitled to them. We lie to our children and convince ourselves that they're too young to understand the truth. We sleep with someone other than our spouse and console ourselves that it's nothing unusual—everybody does it. We cheat on our taxes and think of it as a statement against bloated, greedy government. Seldom do we admit the truth, even to ourselves, and say, "Yes, I'm stealing these office supplies" or "Yes, I'm lying to my children" or "Yes, I'm committing adultery" or "Yes, I am illegally keeping for myself what I know belongs to the state."

Justifying our guilt may allow us to carry on "life as normal" for a while, but reality always wins in the end. Then all our justifications evaporate into thin, wispy clouds of deceit. And there's nothing "heroic" about that.

2. We can try to deny that any guilt exists.

A second way we try to deal with guilt is to deny that it exists. We don't try to justify what we have done; instead we simply maintain that no guilt should attach to our actions. As the infamous bumper sticker proclaims, SCREW GUILT.

Increasingly this seems to be the route our culture is taking. More and more we say, "I am going to do this thing, and there's nothing wrong with it"—even though the Bible and thousands of years of human civilization beg to differ.

I have grown weary of celebrities parading their wickedness across our television screens while boasting about their latest public abominations. I fear for a culture that mocks virgins and chastity while it celebrates studs and perversity. I read the prophet Jeremiah's phrase that "they do not even know how to blush" (Jeremiah 6:15), and I think he must be walking our streets.

We have lost our sense of shame. We denounce guilt, we reject it, we banish it to medieval dungeons, we deny it and we scorn it— and yet it eats away at what's left of our consciences, like a rat growing fatter as it gorges on an unlimited supply of cheese (blue, to match our surly dispositions).

But denying guilt doesn't make it go away. It only makes it tougher and denser and more likely to shatter our ramshackle egos into a thousand prickly shards. The apostle Paul says it's possible to "sear" our consciences "as with a hot iron" (1 Timothy 4:2). No wonder our mental institutions are bursting at the seams.

3. We can resolve our guilt by allowing Jesus Christ to forgive us.

I heard a story the other day. A man dies and arrives in eternity and faces a boring usher. The usher says, "Look, buddy, there's a long line behind you. You've got to hurry up and make a decision. Left door goes to hell, right door goes to heaven. Pick which one you want."

The guy replies, "I have a choice?"

"Yes," the usher says impatiently, "you have a choice."

"But wait!" the man cries. "I need to be forgiven! I want to go to heaven, but I need somebody to forgive me first. I don't deserve heaven."

The usher shakes his head and says, "Look, pal, we don't have time. People keep dying. The line is long. Left door hell, right door heaven. Make your choice and get on with it."

The guy goes left.

Why?

Somewhere inside, all of us feel that there is right and wrong (even if we don't know what they are). We know that right is to be commended and wrong is to be punished. We know that we deserve to be punished. We also know that we need to be forgiven. Now, will someone please forgive us?

That is exactly why Jesus Christ came into the world. As the apostle Paul wrote, "Here is a trustworthy saying that deserves full acceptance: Christ Jesus came into the world to save sinners" (1 Timothy 1:15). Jesus Himself put it like this: "The Son of Man did not come to be served, but to serve, and to give his life as a ransom for many" (Matthew 20:28).

We do not have to live with guilt. We do not have to deny it or justify it. Through Christ, we can resolve it once for all. And we can go to the right in the heavenly line and not to the left. How? We can take four simple steps to rid ourselves of personal guilt and receive God's offer of complete forgiveness.

• *Admit that your guilt is deserved.*

Guilt comes from sin, and the apostle John wrote, "If we confess our sins, he is faithful and just and will forgive us our sins and purify us from all unrighteousness" (1 John 1:9). The first step to receiving God's forgiveness is to admit we have dishonored and displeased Him.

Now, there's a difference between seeking forgiveness and asking to be excused. C. S. Lewis pointed out this distinction many years ago. Much of the time when we say, "Please forgive me," what we're really asking is, "Please excuse me." We're not asking for forgiveness, but to be excused. We don't want to admit that what we did was wrong; we simply want to be let off the hook.

But God does not offer to excuse us; He offers to forgive us. And the first step toward receiving His forgiveness is to admit that we have sinned. No excuses, no justifications. We simply say, "Lord, I have offended You by my actions. I have chosen to displease You, and I have dishonored Your holy name by what I have done. I have sinned."

Once we have humbled ourselves and done that, we are ready for the next step toward receiving the forgiveness offered to us by Jesus Christ.

• *Alter your attitude toward sin.*

The Bible says that for God to forgive us, we need to repent. That means that we must not only admit we have sinned, but also change our attitude toward our sinful actions. We are not only sorry for them, but we determine to turn from them and leave them behind. As the apostle Peter said in one of his first sermons after Jesus rose from the dead, "Repent, then, and turn to God, so that your sins may be wiped out, that times of refreshing may come from the Lord" (Acts 3:19).

We say, "Father, I am sorry for my sins. I do not want to dishonor You anymore. I no longer want to engage in the kind of behavior that made it necessary for Jesus Christ to die on the cross. I want to turn from my old, sinful lifestyle and begin a way of life that brings honor to Your holy name." Then we are ready for the next step.

• *Accept God's free offer of salvation in His Son, Jesus Christ.*

The apostle John wrote of Jesus, "To all who received him, to those who believed in his name, he gave the right to become children of God" (John 1:12). And the apostle Paul declared, "If you confess with your mouth, 'Jesus is Lord,' and believe in your heart that God raised him from the dead, you will be saved" (Romans 10:9).

This is the good news I announced to Jim when he called "Night Talk," full of remorse for the way he had abused his family.

"I think the hardest thing right now is that I'm feeling a tremendous amount of guilt," he told me. "I feel that I've really let my wife and my children down, as well as the other people who have known me and who have tried to help me in the past. I let them all down. It's very hard to deal with the guilt."

"It is," I agreed. "But you cannot carry that on your conscience forever. I believe that you are truly repentant. You're not justifying yourself or explaining away your actions. You're being honest enough to say, 'I've let them down. I've hurt them. I've insulted them, not only my family but God.' That is repentance. The Bible says, 'If we confess our sins, He is faithful and just to forgive us our sins and to cleanse us from all unrighteousness.' You need to settle this before we can talk about tomorrow and all the tomorrows yet to come. Are you truly broken and repentant?"

"Yes, I think I am," he replied.

"You remember that King David in the Old Testament committed adultery with the wife of one of his soldiers," I reminded him. "And when he learned that the woman was pregnant, he had the soldier killed to cover up his immorality. For a whole year he thought he'd hidden his sin—but then a prophet came, pointed a bony finger at him, and said, 'You have done this and that.' Then King David of Israel fell on his face and repented on the spot.

"This is what he said in Psalm Fifty-one: 'Have mercy on me, O God, according to your unfailing love. According to your great compassion, blot out my transgressions.' This is the plea of a guilty man, and you should make Psalm Fifty-one your plea, Jim. It says, 'Wash away all my sin. Cleanse me from my guilt.' Later it says, 'Cleanse me with hyssop and I will be clean. Wash me and I shall be whiter than snow. Let me hear joy and gladness. Let the bones that you have crushed rejoice. Hide your face from my sins and blot out all my iniquity.' Then David pleads, 'Create in me, O God, a pure heart and renew a steadfast spirit within me.' And finally in verse seventeen it says, 'The sacrifices of God are a broken spirit, a broken and contrite heart, O God, you will not despise.'

"Jim, if you say, 'O God, it is awful what I did. Not only did I let them down. Not only is my reputation down in the mud. But my girls—I abused them. I hurt them. I have done something really terrible.' When you do that, God says, 'Your sins and evil deeds I will remember no more.'

"Now, that doesn't mean that forever afterward you act indifferent to your sin. You must ask your family for forgiveness. Confess it all. But you don't have to keep bringing it up to others. That behavior is self-destructive and will not let you mature or grow. You should always be grateful to the Lord and always tell the world, 'I have done awful things'—but don't go into details. People don't need to know the details. Never hide the fact that you were a terrible sinner, but emphasize that you have been wonderfully forgiven. On the other hand, don't do what I call 'sanitizing your testimony.' Don't try to act as if you were just a wonderful guy who made a few minor mistakes. What you did was a horrible thing, but the blood of Christ cleansed you. Now you're a new man. And you can begin to walk in purity and holiness."

This is such good news, that many people have trouble believing it. That was the problem with Sue, who called the program a couple of years ago, full of guilt. She said her husband had been ignoring her for six months, and one night she drank too much and slept with a married co-worker, a longtime family friend.

She sobbed. "I know I broke one of God's laws. I know that God would never, ever forgive me for this."

"I want to contradict you," I said. "God *will* forgive you."

"But I broke one of his Commandments," she insisted.

"Exactly," I replied. "But why do you think Jesus Christ died on the cross? Do you think He came to forgive only perfect people? Who do you think He came to forgive?"

"I know I'm not perfect," she admitted.

"Of course," I said, "but neither am I. I haven't committed that specific sin, but I, too, sin against the Lord. When Christ died on the cross, He died for lawbreakers. Jesus Christ died on the cross for you, and He gave his life for you, and on the cross He did a perfect work. Probably fifty percent of Americans have committed adultery; I wish that all of them had the sense of guilt you have. Because if they did, they could be forgiven and bounce back and begin to walk with God. I am glad that you feel rotten about what you did, because it *is* wrong; it is a serious sin. Jesus shed His blood so that you could be forgiven and restored. And then you can serve the living and true God. At this moment you feel guilty, and rightly so. You feel 'I'm finished.' But that's not true."

"But I failed Him," she wailed. "I just don't know what to do. I'm devastated."

Then I pointed Sue to the promise of Hebrews 9:14—"The blood of Christ, who through the eternal Spirit offered himself unblemished to God, will cleanse our consciences from acts that lead to death, so that we may serve the living God"—but she couldn't grasp it.

"That's fine," she replied, "but I just don't feel cleansed."

I explained that God is faithful even when we're not, and then I said, "Sue, do you want to be forgiven, or do you want to wallow in misery for the rest of your life?"

"No," she said, "I want to be forgiven!"

"If you want to be forgiven, I can help you right now," I answered. "But you must *want* to be forgiven. There is only one way out. You must confess your sins directly to the Lord, and then ask Him to forgive you. And He will! He does things right.

"How do you settle adultery right? You confess your sin. You accept the forgiveness of God. Don't go through this baloney of 'I can't forgive myself.' No, you can't forgive yourself. No one can. God forgives us, and we accept His forgiveness and we are forgiven. God will say to you from His Word, 'Woman, I forgive you because I died in your place for that dirty little sin.' From then on you are free, as though you had never committed that sin. The Lord will forgive you and cleanse you, and you can walk in freedom. You will be free in Christ to walk with God."

Sue finally understood, and by the end of our conversation she had found release from the guilt that had been crushing her.

• *Allow peace to reign in your heart.*

It's one thing to admit your guilt, repent of your sin, and accept God's forgiveness. It's another to allow the peace of God to quiet your cleansed heart. As the apostle Paul wrote, you must *"Let* the peace of Christ rule in your hearts" (Colossians 3:15).

Twenty-seven-year-old Rose called the program one night, deeply distressed over her imminent third divorce. She was first married at seventeen, a union that lasted all of three days. She described numerous medical problems and said she was taking Prozac for depression. She finished by admitting, "Something is bothering me."

"Your conscience is bothering you," I replied. "Your emotions are disturbed. What you need, is the peace of God in your heart. Forget men for a while; you should have had your fill. Three is plenty for any woman in a lifetime. I think you need to start over again. You're young enough. You're intelligent. You speak very clearly. What's missing is not more love from a man; what you need is the love of God in your soul.

"Though you have botched up your young life quite a bit, the Lord still loves you. The Bible says, 'Even while we were sinners, Christ died for us' [Romans 5:8]. He loves you just as you are. He doesn't say, 'Rose, shape up, be a good girl, and then I'll love you.' God says to you, 'Rose, let Me love you. Let Me come into your life.'

"Christ died on the cross to forgive your sins, and He will forgive all this messy life that you've made for yourself. He'll forgive it all. He'll forgive you for bouncing around from one man to another, and you will be a new woman—if you open your heart to Christ.

"Then you will have the peace of God, and you will not struggle the way you're struggling now. You won't feel like an emotional yo-yo, up and down, up and down. You will enjoy a more steady life. The prophet Ezekiel writes, 'The Lord says, 'I will take away the heart of stone and give you a heart of flesh' (Ezekiel 36:26). The Lord will change your very heart. He will give you a tender heart, a pure heart, a heart that loves God. You can bury your past forever at the feet of Jesus Christ and live, finally, at peace."

That's what God does when He forgives our sin and our guilt. He doesn't merely pave over the problem or excuse our guilt; He resolves it, once for all. When we look at the cross of Christ, we see the only certain and permanent way to be free of the crushing burden of guilt and to live as free men and women. Jesus died and rose again to free us from the bondage of guilt and sin.

FREE AT LAST

The message of the Gospel is Good News to all who are drowning in an ocean of guilt. It is a message of hope, a message of forgiveness and peace and life. The Gospel of Jesus Christ cuts through all the layers of guilt and defense mechanisms and presents us with God's offer of true psychological and spiritual freedom. When we read the Bible, we are convicted of sin, but its main theme is Good News.

If we want it, we can be forgiven. We do not have to choose the line to the left and spend eternity in our guilt and shame, as did the man in the story I told earlier. Jesus offers us freedom from guilt and an eternity of life with Him in heaven.

Yes, we sin. Yes, we are guilty. But there is forgiveness in Jesus Christ!

Anyone to the right?

"But how, Luis?" you may be asking.

By choosing to open the door of your heart to Christ.

"What do you mean?"

Jesus said it best: "Here I am! I stand at the door and knock. If anyone hears my voice and opens the door, I will come in and eat with him, and him with me" (Revelation 3:20). In other words, He's inviting you and me to a party—that never ends!

Have you heard Jesus speaking to your own heart? If so, why not stop right now, where you are, and in the quietness of your heart talk to Him?

I suggest that you pray the following prayer of commitment:

"Lord, I come before You humbly, in the midst of my heartache and sorrow. Yes, please forgive my sins. Thank You that Jesus died on the cross

to cleanse my heart and rose again to give me new eternal life. Thank You that now I can enjoy the sure hope of heaven. I love You, Lord, and will live for You all the days of my life. Amen."

If that's your prayer, you've made the right choice. You're clean. Forgiven. At peace with God forever![1]

---

[1] If you've just committed your life to Jesus Christ, please write to me. I'll be glad to correspond with you and send you a free copy of my book, *Your New Life with Christ*. It's yours free for the asking. Or perhaps you would like further counsel and prayer on experiencing God's forgiveness. Again, please feel free to write. My address is Luis Palau, P.O. Box 1173, Portland, Oregon 97207, U.S.A. E-mail: palau@palau.org.

PART
THREE

13

THE SUN
STILL SHINES

The other day I was thinking about Duane, the good friend I described in Chapter 6 whose funeral I attended a while back. I already miss him a lot, and to ease my sorrow I started to leaf through a hymnal. Songwriters often wonderfully put into words what we're feeling and thinking, and I soon found an old song that greatly lifted my spirits.

"When by His grace I shall look on His face, that will be glory, be glory for me," wrote Fanny Crosby, a nineteenth-century hymn writer who in her long lifetime composed more than nine thousand poems and songs, a third of which were published. Fanny's old song encouraged me, not only because it reminded me that sorrow will one day be swallowed up in joy, but also because its very existence shouts that the sun still shines even when dark clouds obscure its radiance.

You see, it meant everything to Fanny that she would see her Savior's face, because her world lacked any faces at all. She was blind from the time she was six weeks old.

Fanny wasn't born blind, but in her first month of life she developed an eye infection. A local man who claimed to know something about medicine put a hot poultice on her red and inflamed eyes. Fanny's parents worried about this treatment, but the man insisted that it would draw out the baby's infection. When the poultices were removed, however, it became clear that permanent damage had been done. Fanny was blind. Her corneas had been badly burned, leaving ugly white scars on both eyes.

Seven months later, tragedy struck again. Fanny's father, John Crosby, caught a bad chill while working in a cold November rain. He died within days, leaving behind a twenty-one-year-old widow and an eight-month-old blind baby. Fanny and her mother, Mercy, were plunged into deep poverty, and Mercy hired herself out as a domestic worker to pay the bills. Many nights she returned home overwhelmed with life and collapsed weeping on her rough cot. It was then that her own mother, Eunice, would place a hand on her daughter's shoulder and quote the Puritan proverb "What can't be cured can be endured." Fanny must have heard this proverb often as a child, because even into her nineties she continued to quote it to anyone who came to her in trouble.

Fanny was not totally blind; she could see a little color and could distinguish night from day. Although she came to be known as "the blind poetess" or "the blind hymn writer," she hated both titles. When people said to her, "How terrible it is that you were blinded as a baby," she graciously but instantly told them that she considered it no tragedy at all. Bernard Ruffin, Fanny's biographer, wrote:

> *Far from feeling self-pity, Fanny felt that on the whole it was a special gift of God that she was blind. She often said, "It was the best thing that could have happened to me," and "How in the world could I have lived such a helpful life as I have lived had I not been blind?" She felt that she would never have had the opportunity for education had she not been blind, and had she not gone to the Institution in New York [The New York Institution for the Blind] she would not have had the contacts to enable her to write hymns for a nationally known publishing firm. Moreover, she felt that sight must be a distraction, and she attributed her great powers of concentration to blindness. She also felt that lack of sight enabled her to develop a wonderful memory and enhanced her appeal as a speaker. It created a bond of sympathy between*

her and her audiences that made them more receptive to the gospel message. . . .

Many wondered whether she harbored some bitterness toward the mountebank who prescribed the poultices that burned out her eyes. She would always say, very tenderly, "Don't blame the doctor. He is probably dead before this time. But if I could meet him, I would tell him that he unwittingly did me the greatest favor in the world."[1]

This was no new conviction for Fanny, nor a position developed over long years of hardship. Even as an eight-year-old she wrote,

Oh, what a happy child I am,
  Although I cannot see!
I am resolved that in this world
  Contented I will be!

How many blessings I enjoy
  That other people don't!
To weep or sigh because I'm blind,
  I cannot—nor I won't.[2]

Now, *that's* how you turn tragedy into triumph! Although Fanny couldn't see the sun, she could feel its warmth. And she was happy to be alive.

Perhaps such a fiercely positive outlook was easier in some respects for Fanny's generation than it is for our own. As biographer Ruffin wrote of Fanny's time, "Death and sickness and pain were taken for granted; they were not seen as an absurd intrusion upon one's existence. It was considered unnatural and downright foolish to assume that earthly joys last forever, and preparing for death was deemed of prime importance. The big question for the average person of the 1820s was not 'Will I die?' or 'When will I die?' or 'How will I die?' The big question was, 'When I die, where will I go?'"[3]

---

[1] Bernard Ruffin, *Fanny Crosby* (Pilgrim Press, 1976), 219, 220.
[2] Ruffin, 28.
[3] Ruffin, 29.

And Fanny had a lot of opportunity to think about death. She was too young to remember her father's demise, but she could never forget the death of her own child, who died in infancy. This was the heartbreak of Fanny's life, and she almost never spoke about it; we don't even know if the child was a boy or a girl. Years later she wrote a hymn called "Safe in the Arms of Jesus," which she always said she wrote especially for mothers who had lost children. Ruffin begins his biography with a touching story about this woman and her song:

> The year is 1910. The place is Perth Amboy, New Jersey. A hackman stops to pick up two passengers. One is a middle-aged clergyman; the other is a withered old crone, apparently blind, ravaged and wasted almost beyond belief, bent nearly double with age. But as the coach jolts along en route to the railroad depot, the hackman becomes aware that there is something unusual about this ancient woman, seemingly straight out of one of Grimms' Fairy Tales. She is speaking to the clergyman. Her voice is not dry and quavering, as one might be led from her appearance to expect, but it is clear and high and mellow and young. Far from the senility that one might expect in one so venerable (she must be more than a hundred!), the lady's mind is as fresh and young as her voice. She evidently is a woman of great intellect and refinement. She and the clergyman are discussing some point of theology. The coachman listens intently to the wit and wisdom the old lady displays. When it becomes obvious that the driver is paying more attention to what she is saying than to the road, the minister speaks up.
> "This is Fanny Crosby, the hymn writer," he says. The hackman is stunned. He stops his horse, takes off his hat, and weeps openly. Getting himself together, he proceeds to the depot, where he searches for a policeman and finds one. He introduces the old woman to him. "This is Miss Fanny Crosby that wrote 'Safe in the Arms of Jesus.' I want you to help this young man get her safely to the train."
> The cop is stunned. "I sure will," he says. Then he says, falteringly, to the little old lady, "We sang your hymn, 'Safe in the Arms of Jesus,' last week—at my little girl's funeral."
> As he looks at the ground with reddened and shining eyes, "Aunt Fanny" takes his enormous arm in her skinny hands and

says, with great feeling and tenderness, "My boy—I call all po-
licemen and railroad men 'my boys,' they take such good care of
me wherever I go—God bless your dear heart! You shall have my
prayers! And tell your dear wife that your dear little girl is 'Safe
in the Arms of Jesus.' " With these words, the constable broke
down and wept openly.[4]

Fanny Crosby died on February 12, 1915, just a month short of
her ninety-fifth birthday. Her funeral was reportedly the largest
ever in Bridgeport, Connecticut, surpassing even that of circus czar
P. T. Barnum. People stood for blocks to file past her coffin.

And all to pay tribute to a little blind woman who refused to
believe that the sun had gone dark just because she couldn't see
it!

She did think about seeing, however. One of her later hymns,
"My Savior First of All," looked forward to the day when she
would at last see her Savior. One stanza in that song says, "When
my lifework is ended and I cross the swelling tide,/When the
bright and glorious morning I shall see,/I shall know my Redeemer
when I reach the other side,/And His smile will be the first to
welcome me."

Fanny Crosby knew how to focus on all that was good in her
life, and that habit helped her to avoid a negative, morose perspective. She understood—as we must—that there truly is much to be
thankful for, even when tragedy strikes. Like her, we must recognize that the sun has shined on us throughout our lives, whether or
not we can see its brilliant rays knifing through the clouds.

A GOOD DOSE OF REALITY

To recognize that the sun still shines we do not have to pretend
that dark clouds never gather. The Bible is brutally honest here.
One of the most graphic examples of this is found in the little Old
Testament book of Lamentations.

Get a dictionary and you will see that a lamentation is "the act
of expressing grief"—and the book of Lamentations, traditionally
ascribed to Jeremiah ("the weeping prophet"), certainly fits that

[4] Ruffin, 13.

definition. It is five chapters of sobs, moans, loud wailing, laments, and groans. Jeremiah surveys the destruction of ancient Jerusalem, ruined by the invading Babylonian army, and he lets loose with one long wail of grief.

In the first three chapters he speaks of "exile," of "destruction," of slaughtered soldiers and starving children and demolished walls and fire everywhere. The stench of death and rotting flesh hangs in the smoky air—and the prophet is beside himself. He knows that the city was ravaged because of its sin—he has been predicting it for years, despite a hostile audience—but he still can't quite accept the truth. And he wonders where God could be in all of this misery.

"I am the man who has seen affliction by the rod of [God's] wrath," he says. "He has driven me away and made me walk in darkness rather than light; indeed, he has turned his hand against me again and again, all day long. He has made my skin and my flesh grow old and has broken my bones. He has besieged me and surrounded me with bitterness and hardship. He has made me dwell in darkness like those long dead. He has walled me in so I cannot escape; he has weighed me down with chains. . . . He has broken my teeth with gravel; he has trampled me in the dust. I have been deprived of peace; I have forgotten what prosperity is. So I say, 'My splendor is gone and all that I had hoped from the LORD.' I remember my affliction and my wandering, the bitterness and the gall. I well remember them, and my soul is downcast within me" (Lamentations 3:1–7,16–20).

A deeper expression of anguish is hard to imagine. The sky is an iron slab of solid black, and Jeremiah can see no ray of sunshine peeking through the tiniest crack.

And yet he knows that the sun still shines.

"Yet this I call to mind and therefore I have hope," he continues. "Because of the LORD'S great love we are not consumed, for his compassions never fail. They are new every morning; great is your faithfulness. I say to myself, 'The LORD is my portion; therefore I will wait for him" (Lamentations 3:21–24).

Even when the sun was blotted out of his vision, even when multiplied tragedies dogged every step he took, even when all hope seemed extinguished—Jeremiah looked up and realized that the sun *was* shining (though he couldn't see it), that a faithful companion also walked with him (though he couldn't see him), and that hope had not perished (though he didn't know when it would reappear). Jeremiah refused to give up on life, even though in the last two chapters of his book the storm clouds return and he wanders in darkness for a time once more.

The Bible never claims that life with God will always be rosy. But it does insist that when roses bloom, they do so at God's command. And it does proclaim that even in tragedy, God walks with His children.

Jesus said much the same thing in the New Testament. When His disciples heard their master say He was going away to die on the cross, they were both confused and alarmed. "I tell you the truth, you will weep and mourn while the world rejoices," Jesus told them. "You will grieve, but your grief will turn to joy. A woman giving birth to a child has pain because her time has come; but when her baby is born she forgets the anguish because of her joy that a child is born into the world. So with you: Now is your time of grief, but I will see you again and you will rejoice, and no one will take away your joy" (John 16:20–22).

You will grieve . . . no one will take away your joy. Both truths, right up front, right out in the open. Jesus never tries to hide from us the fact that grief and sorrow and tragedy are part of our lot in this life. But at the same time He guarantees that He will lavish upon all His followers a delirious joy that cannot be extinguished. In other words, although dark clouds gather, the sun still shines.

EVERY MORNING IS A NEW OPPORTUNITY TO LIVE

Even when I've had a horrendous day, a worse evening, and I go to bed feeling rotten, I remind myself that the next morning will bring a new day. I try to remember to begin every day by saying, "Thank You, God, that I'm alive."

You may be suffering under burdens I can't imagine. You may be physically disabled or financially wiped out. You may have lost a loved one, or you may be facing imminent death. Life may seem unbearable—*but you're alive!* Life may be awful—*but you're alive!* Even if you're hurting terribly or you can't do what you once did— *you're alive!* So live! Live to the maximum possible for you. Be all that you can be, within your limitations. We all have limitations; but that fact doesn't have to turn us into petrified human beings.

When someone insists on complaining and cursing about something in his or her life, I often say, "Would you rather not have been born? Or is life worth it, despite having to endure some of these things?"

Every morning that we have the strength to open our eyes, we ought to thank God for another day of life and ask Him for the grace and strength to make the most of it. It really is a great gift.

YOU DON'T HAVE TO FACE TOMORROW ALONE

Life goes on, whether you've suffered a terrible loss or endured a horrific surgery or lost a child. Tomorrow is coming, and we have to face it. *But we don't have to face it alone.*

One of God's favorite promises throughout the Bible is "I will be with you." He made that promise to Abraham, to Moses, to David, and to scores of other men and women throughout both testaments. It is tremendously significant that Jesus' last recorded words to us in the book of Matthew are "Surely I am with you always, to the very end of the age" (Matthew 28:20).

Tomorrow is coming, but we don't have to face it alone. If we try to face it without God, only disaster awaits. But if we face tomorrow with the presence of God through Jesus Christ and His Spirit, we have hope and the divine promise of a bright new beginning.

But God doesn't promise us His presence only! That would be enough, but He is not content to leave it at that. Throughout the Bible He promises to do good to His people in a wild variety of ways. Five of His most precious promises are these:

1. *"The Lord is near to all who call on him, to all who call on him in truth. He fulfills the desires of those who fear him; he hears their cry and saves them"* (Psalm 145:18–19).

To whom is the Lord near, according to the psalmist? To everyone who calls on the Lord "in truth." How do you call on Him in truth? By admitting your need and your sin, and by placing your trust in Him. And what does He promise to do when He hears your call? He answers your cry and saves you!

2. *"Come to me, all you who are weary and burdened, and I will give you rest. Take my yoke upon you and learn from me, for I am gentle and humble in heart, and you will find rest for your souls"* (Matthew 11:28–29).

All of us require rest, and here Jesus promises to give us all the rest we need. Are you weary? Burdened? Then Jesus invites you to come to Him and to learn from Him. You needn't worry that you'll be turned away, because He is gentle and humble and offers you all the rest you need. There is no reason to continue bearing burdens too heavy for us. Jesus has promised to lighten our load if only we will come to Him.

3. *"I am the resurrection and the life. He who believes in me will live, even though he dies; and whoever lives and believes in me will never die"* (John 11:25, 26).

Jesus Christ conquered death when He arose from the grave after His crucifixion, and now He invites you to join Him in that victory by placing your faith in Him. He offers you eternal life if only you will believe in Him. Nothing to buy. Nothing to earn. Nothing to strive for. Simply believe that He died on the cross for your sins, affirm that He rose from the tomb alive after being dead for three days, and confess Him as your Lord and Savior. That's all He asks.

4. *"No eye has seen, no ear has heard, no mind has conceived what God has prepared for those who love him"* (1 Corinthians 2:9).

Some of God's promises are so spectacular, so astonishing, so thrilling, that images and words and even concepts fall impossibly short of conveying their full import. Whatever God has planned for His children is so great that it is simply beyond their comprehension. But note, this promise is only for those who love Him. Do you love God as your Father? Do you love His Son, Jesus Christ? Jesus said, "If God were your Father, you would love me, for I came from God" (John 8:42). If that describes you, then you have an ironclad promise from God that will make you say, as it did the apostle Paul, "I consider that our present sufferings are not worth comparing with the glory that will be revealed in us" (Romans 8:18).

5. *"God has said, 'Never will I leave you; never will I forsake you.' So we say with confidence, 'The Lord is my helper; I will not be afraid. What can man do to me?"* *(Hebrews 13:5–6).*

Man can do a lot of things to us—except the only lasting thing. Jesus said, "Do not be afraid of those who kill the body but cannot kill the soul. Rather, be afraid of the One who can destroy both soul and body in hell" (Matthew 10:28). If we have been reconciled to God through faith in His Son, Jesus Christ, then no one and nothing can ever separate us from the love of God (Romans 8:38–39). We can live confidently and unafraid in this world, knowing that God Himself is our helper. He will *never* leave us or forsake us, not even when calamities or tragedies strike. And that takes the teeth out of fear.

START EACH DAY WITH GOD'S PERSPECTIVE

I need to start each day with God, and I try to look at the events about to unfold from God's perspective. That's essential when things are going our way—but how much more so when tragedy strikes and death touches our home!

What does it mean to start each day from God's perspective? It means we take the long view. It means we place our full trust and confidence in God, even when our world appears to be falling apart and the sun has stopped shining. It means we "rejoice with those who rejoice and mourn with those who mourn" (Romans 12:15). It means we face life with courage and integrity, knowing that God wins in the end. And it means we remember we are only in Act Two of a three-act play. Tragedy may strut and prance in the spotlight right now, but when the final curtain falls, hope will retire to the shadows and victory will stand straight and tall at center stage.

A BETTER DAY IS COMING

According to the Bible, a better day is coming in which storm clouds disappear forever and day never turns to night. This new day is as sure as the resurrection of Christ, and that means it's no illusion and no fantasy. A real day is coming in which our fondest dreams come true and all pain and fear and suffering are exiled forever.

Present tragedies may make it seem as if life is all over, but it isn't. There is a future promised by God Almighty, and it is glorious. And it is possible to live courageously and faithfully *right now* in light of this delightful future. This is not "pie in the sky in the great 'by and 'by," but is more like sampling the Great King's banquet tables as they are piled high with mile after unending mile of the tastiest, most succulent, healthiest dishes offered anywhere in the universe.

Tragedy makes life hard; it does not make it hopeless. As long as God is in our present and our future, there is more than hope. There is life, and "pleasures at his right hand forevermore" (Psalm 16:11).

IT DOES NO GOOD TO
LIVE IN THE PAST

With a great future guaranteed to believers in Christ by a loving God who cannot lie, who would choose to live in the past? Sadly, many do.

When you live in the past, you sacrifice hope. You cannot enjoy every day for the pleasures it brings. As painful as your loss or suffering may be, you don't have to live in either of the twin, sunless worlds of "What if . . . ?" or "Why me?" Thousands of hurting people have chosen to be happy. As the eight-year-old Fanny Crosby wrote, "To weep or sigh because I'm blind,/I cannot—nor I won't." Choose to make the best of everything. Choose to redeem your present circumstances. Decide that hope will win.

Nobody wants to be around men or women who live in the past—they're boring. And living in the past is depressing. Who wants to spend time with such a shriveled soul?

Sunset Boulevard is a classic 1950 Billy Wilder film starring William Holden and Gloria Swanson. In the picture, Norma Desmond, an aging movie star of the silent era, refuses to accept the new Hollywood of talking pictures. She lives with her Teutonic butler in a cavernous, spooky old mansion crammed full of photos and memorabilia exclusively connected to her late film career. At a set time every week, she and her butler (who we ultimately learn was her director and the first of her three husbands) dim the lights and watch the young Norma perform on-screen. Creepy doesn't begin to describe the scene.

Into this living mausoleum wanders the character played by William Holden, an unemployed scriptwriter. At their first meeting he turns to Norma, dim recognition in his eyes, and says to her, "You used to be big."

"I *am* big," Norma replies in one of Hollywood's great lines. "It's the pictures that got small."

As their relationship descends to ever more bizarre levels, narrator Holden at one point says that Norma Desmond was "still waving proudly to a parade that had long since passed her by," and later, "There's nothing tragic about being fifty—unless you're trying to be twenty-five."

Norma Desmond is the film world's archetypal character stuck in the past. And she's not only boring—by the end of the film she's also a murderer.

Don't live in the past. It's a world without color, without sound, without life. Don't make your pain worse by pulling a Norma Desmond. You can't afford it, and neither can those around you.

GET RID OF BITTERNESS

The sun is shining, but you won't see it if you refuse to forgive the drunk who ran over your child or the doctor who made a mistake or the contractor who failed to do his job. If you won't forgive the ones who hurt you, you're not only destroying every ounce of your joy, you are embittering everyone around you.

Just the other day I heard about a man eaten up with bitterness because he cannot forgive the ones responsible for taking his daughter's life. He has three healthy sons and a capable wife, but they might as well not exist. His daughter—his youngest child and the apple of his eye—was killed years ago in an alcohol-related traffic accident. This father flies into rages at the slightest provocation, refuses to attend family functions, and seldom leaves his house. When he does so, the routine is always the same. At the front door he pauses, turns to one corner where he has set up a shrine to his deceased daughter, and says softly, "Good-bye, Susie." Only then will he exit.

If you are going to enjoy the sun that is shining, you have to forgive, or a cloud will always darken the sky over your head. The comedian Buddy Hackett once said, in effect, "I never hold grudges, because while I'm home crying, they're out dancing." He's right. I think unforgiveness and bitterness are a lot like worry. "Worry never robs tomorrow of its sorrow; it only saps today of its strength," said the novelist A. J. Cronin.

Don't allow unforgiveness and bitterness to steal your joy of living. Bitterness is an emotional and spiritual poison that eventually kills its victims. If you're drinking its deadly potion, stop. Yes, people may have hurt you—but why will you allow them to go on hurting you? Confess your unforgiving and bitter heart to the Lord and let Him soften it. Allow Him to restore your joy and return your life to you. The sun really is shining! Why not enjoy it?

THE SUN STILL SHINES

A few days ago, while I was finishing this book, the skies grew dark and threatening over Nashville, Tennessee, and a series of tornadoes touched down in the heart of the city's office district, virtually shutting it down for three days. In the aftermath eight buildings were "red-tagged" as unsafe, and skyscrapers everywhere were patched with plywood and tarpaulins.

Miraculously, no one was killed in Nashville. But property damage was extensive. President Clinton declared six Tennessee counties disaster areas, and experts estimated that it could take more than eight weeks to replace all the glass shattered in the tornadoes. By anyone's standards the devastation in Nashville ranks as a disaster.

But I noted with interest a single line in an Associated Press report about the storm. "Most of the large office towers reopened," it said, "as weekend rains gave way to sunshine."[5]

That's how it is in this world. Storms hit and do their worst, but the sun still shines. We just have to look up and wait for it to reappear.

[5] Marta W. Aldrich, "Nashville, Tenn., Buildings Reopen," The Associated Press, April 20, 1998.

14

"WILL NOT THE JUDGE OF ALL THE EARTH DO RIGHT?"

R abbi Harold Kushner once introduced a class of young people to the story of the Holocaust, the infamous World War II atrocity in which six million Jews perished at the hands of the Nazis. In grisly detail he chronicled the crime, describing the gas chambers and the cattle trains used to deliver Jews to Auschwitz and the other death camps. The students were horrified and outraged—and then he asked them, "Was it wrong for Hitler to do this?"

The students were astonished. Of course it was wrong!

"Who says it's wrong?" he pressed.

"It's just wrong. It's *wrong!*" they answered in animated chorus.

"But says who?" he continued. "The laws that Hitler passed justified it, so legally he was doing the right thing. What makes it wrong? What do you mean by wrong?"

After a lively discussion Kushner impressed on his students that all of us possess an innate sense of right and wrong, implanted in our hearts by God. We instinctively *know* that the systematic murder of six million men, women, boys, and girls is a monstrous evil, despite whatever laws might be passed to give the genocide a veneer of morality. How do we know it's wrong? We just know it.

I think Kushner is right. While I don't believe that our consciences are the final arbiters of right and wrong—it's possible to warp and sear the conscience to such a degree that what is really wrong seems absolutely right—I do firmly believe that we have an innate sense of right and wrong based on our creation in the image of a righteous God. As Paul the apostle wrote:

> *The wrath of God is being revealed from heaven against all the godlessness and wickedness of men who suppress the truth by their wickedness, since what may be known about God is plain to them, because God has made it plain to them. For since the creation of the world God's invisible qualities—his eternal power and divine nature—have been clearly seen, being understood from what has been made, so that men are without excuse (Romans 1:18–20).*

Why are individuals without excuse when they act wickedly, according to the apostle? Because God's eternal power and divine nature can be clearly seen everywhere. And why do we instinctively know that the Holocaust was wrong, according to Rabbi Kushner? Because God implanted a sense of right and wrong within us.

In both cases these men say that our recognition of evil depends on the fact of God's righteous and just character. He is the standard against which all actions are to be judged. He is absolutely just and perfectly righteous. He does not sin and cannot sin. He always does right.

So what does that conviction have to do with this book? Just this: The truth that God is just must shape all of our thinking about the calamities and tragedies of life. *God will always do right.* Without that conviction there is no hope. But with it there is hope both omnipotent and eternal.

SOME REASONS FOR SUFFERING— A REVIEW

So God is just and always does right. But if that's true, then why do seemingly innocent people suffer? Why does God allow babies to be deformed and crippled? Why does He permit young mothers to die of cancer? Why does He seem to do nothing to stop natural disasters that take thousands of lives? How can He sit by and watch youngsters raped, grandmothers beaten, whole families wiped out in fiery accidents?

In short, to borrow a phrase from Rabbi Kushner, why do bad things happen to good people?

We have already discussed several reasons that tragedies befall us. Perhaps it would be good here to briefly review these basic answers.

1. We suffer because we are part of a fallen human race.

Many of the personal disasters that overtake us occur simply because we live in a world out of whack. The Bible explains that when the first human beings decided to rebel against God and disobey His commands, the human race was placed under a curse that will not be lifted until God brings a "day of redemption" sometime in the future. When sin entered the world through Adam and Eve, the perfection of the Garden of Eden exited. Ever since then, the world has not been "right."

The apostle Paul explained that because of sin, "the creation was subjected to frustration" and put into "bondage to decay." In fact, he writes, "the whole creation has been groaning as in the pains of childbirth right up to the present time" (Romans 8:20,21,22).

The words he uses—"frustration" and "bondage" and "decay" and "groaning"—are just another way of saying that in this world we get sick, we die young, we are maimed, we lose loved ones in accidents, we give birth to seriously deformed babies. Is this the way it was meant to be? Certainly not! Is it the way it will always be? Thank God, no! As Paul writes, "we ourselves . . . wait eagerly for our adoption as sons, the redemption of our bodies" (Romans 8:23).

And yet for now, we live on a fallen planet where tragedies happen to good and bad, young and old. As an ancient observer of life noted,

> *The race is not to the swift*
> *or the battle to the strong,*
> *nor does food come to the wise*

> *or wealth to the brilliant*
> *or favor to the learned;*
> *but time and chance happen to them all.*
>
> *Moreover, no man knows when his hour will come:*
> *As fish are caught in a cruel net,*
> *or birds are taken in a snare,*
> *so men are trapped by evil times*
> *that fall unexpectedly on them (Ecclesiastes 9:11,12).*

2. Sometimes we suffer due to our own poor choices.

Some tragedies occur because we make poor and unwise choices. A man who decides to build his house in a flood plain is not committing a grave sin against God, but he is inviting disaster.

In the state of Oregon this past year we have been watching just such a scenario play out. Developers built a row of expensive homes on a sandy bluff overlooking the Pacific coast, and now unforeseen erosion caused by El Niño is threatening to send all of the houses crashing onto the beach below. Local residents have been fond of quoting Jesus' words in Matthew 7, a story about a foolish man who built his house on sand: "The rain came down, the streams rose, and the winds blew and beat against that house, and it fell with a great crash" (Matthew 7:27).

Of course, poor choices can result in far more tragic consequences than the loss of a few homes. Not too long ago I heard of a local girl who died in a car accident. She was a fine young woman who did well in school, sang in the church choir, and largely stayed out of trouble. But the night she died, she chose to get in a car driven by a young man who had been drinking, and when he lost control of the car as it sped along at close to a hundred miles an hour, she was thrown from the vehicle and killed. Did she sin by getting into the car? No. Was she being punished for committing some moral offense? No. She simply made a bad choice and paid for it with her life. Tragic, but preventable.

3. Sometimes we suffer because of personal rebellion.

As you think back through the stories in this book, you will probably begin to notice a common theme in many of them: They describe tragedies caused by human sin and rebellion. The hurts of people scarred by divorce, incest, rape, murder, drunk drivers, war, abortion, greed, promiscuity, and countless other forces are really caused by human sin.

Is it fair to blame God for the horrors inflicted by humanity? I don't think so. We must own up to the fact that many of our troubles are created by personal rebellion, whether our own or that of others.

And then, too, I must (very carefully) say something that I know won't be popular. It is biblically accurate to maintain that *some* human suffering is a divine punishment for sin. Some tragedies—and heaven will reveal them, if we still want to know when we get there—are definite punishments for breaking God's moral order. In biblical terms, we reap what we sow. The apostle Paul writes, "The sins of some men are obvious, reaching the place of judgment ahead of them; the sins of others trail behind them" (1 Timothy 5:24).

Occasionally we see this principle at work in the Gospels. In perhaps the most clear instance, Jesus tells a man whom he has just healed, "See, you are well again. Stop sinning or something worse may happen to you" (John 5:14). So some affliction can be a punishment for personal sin.

On the other hand, it is impossible for us mere mortals to say whether a man or woman has been afflicted because he or she has sinned. Beware of people who claim to have such knowledge! In the Old Testament book of Job, three of Job's friends continually accuse him of sin and point to his deep suffering as proof positive of their claim. Yet at the end of that book God calls one of these "friends" on the carpet and says to him, "I am angry with you and your two friends, because you have not spoken of me what is right, as my servant Job has. . . . My servant Job will pray for you, and I will accept his prayer and not deal with you according to your folly" (Job 42:7,8).

Bottom line: It is impossible for any of us to say, "Whenever something like that happens, it's a punishment from God."

4. Often we just don't know why we suffer.

Several years ago a talented, bright, and effective campus evangelist named Paul Little wrote a bestselling book called *How to*

Give Away Your Faith. In an excellent section of the book describing the seven biggest questions that skeptical college students ask about Christianity, he answers the question "If God is all-good and all-powerful, why do the innocent suffer? Why are some babies born blind or mentally defective or deformed? Why are wars allowed? Why . . . ?" Little continues:

> *Either God is all-good, but He is not powerful enough to eliminate disease and disaster; or He is all-powerful, but He is not all-good and therefore He does not end all evil.*
>
> *Once again I think we must admit our partial ignorance. We don't have the full explanation of the origin and problem of evil because God has chosen to reveal only a part of it to us. We are clearly told, though, that God created the universe perfect. Man was given the freedom to obey God or disobey. Evil came into the universe through man's disobedience. Because of the pattern of the universe, man's actions are not limited to himself but always involve other people. Because man disobeyed and broke God's law, evil pervades the universe.*
>
> *As we discuss this question, we mustn't overlook the presence of evil in every one of us. Many people ask, "Why doesn't God step in and get rid of evil? Why doesn't He stomp out war?" They do not realize that if God exercised judgment uniformly, not one of us would survive. Suppose God were to decree, "At midnight tonight, all evil will be stamped out of the universe." Which of us would be here at 1:00 A.M.?[1]*

It's good food for thought, isn't it? I think it would be fascinating to get Little on the phone and interview him to hear more of his views. Probe a little deeper. Dig for more insights.

Except I can't do that. He's no longer around. At the height of his effective ministry, in 1975, Little was killed in a car crash. Why? Why would God take him out of this world when he was helping to direct so many people to heaven? I don't know. I simply have to agree with Little himself: "Once again I think we must admit our partial ignorance."

[1] Paul Little, *How to Give Away Your Faith* (Downers Grove, Ill.: InterVarsity Press, 1966), 71, 72.

The truth is, some questions are unanswerable from our earth-bound perspective. For example, I know a godly woman, the daughter of a pastor, who married the student-body president of a Christian school (who doubled as the Sunday-school superintendent for his church). This woman thought she had married the epitome of Christian commitment. And yet shortly after their marriage he became an alcoholic who stole all her money, abused her physically, then lied about it. Why did God not allow this woman to see this tragedy ahead of time? How could He allow it to go on for decades? I don't know. And when you ask her, she doesn't even look for an answer. She simply keeps walking with her Lord, weeping as she goes.

Or take another example. Just the other day the wife of a friend of mine died suddenly, without warning. She went in for minor surgery, the doctor couldn't stop her bleeding, and she was gone in an hour. There was no explanation. We were all appalled. I was traveling at the time but immediately called the husband, a friend of mine for forty years. In a voice filled with utter devastation he said wearily, "Boy, Luis, I wish you were here to give me a big Latin hug."

How can we explain something like that? I can't. In cases like this the only thing I can do is to trust that God makes no mistakes, that He has a purpose in everything He does, and that He will always do what is right—whether we understand it or not.

WHY DOESN'T GOD DO SOMETHING?

When we ponder human tragedy, we must be careful to avoid getting stuck on the single question "Where was God when . . . ?" We always seem to want to lay the blame for inaction at the feet of God—but I think we need to lay a high percentage of blame at our own feet.

Somebody once asked Jean-Paul Sartre, the French philosopher, "Where was God when the Nazis were about to overrun Europe?" Sartre replied, "Where was man?"

I suppose he meant, why didn't the Western powers stop Hitler before he really got going? Why didn't they take action sooner, when they knew the danger but before the Nazis could ravage the Continent? Indeed, *where was man?*

And where is he today?

I can't help but notice that we tend to fault God for not acting to prevent disaster when it is often fully in our own power to do so. We ask, "Where was God when . . . ?" as we sip strawberry lemonades at poolside.

Joni Eareckson Tada is a friend of mine who suffers from quadriplegia. She is well acquainted with suffering and tragedy, having broken her neck at age seventeen in a diving accident. She has thought long and deeply on God's role in human suffering, and in a book titled *The God Who Weeps* she writes:

> *God's heart intent is to alleviate suffering. He is bending over backward to make it happen. God is moving heaven and earth to dry the tear, lighten the load, ease the burden, take away the pain, stop the wars, halt the violence, cure the disease, heal the heartbroken, mend the marriage. . . .*
>
> *He rallies us to his noble cause, but we fall behind. If God is weeping, it is because he has made his heart intent regarding suffering abundantly clear, but few—even of his own people—are moved into action. We aren't listening.*
>
> *For day after day [my people] seek me out; they seem eager to know my ways, as if they were a nation that does what is right and has not forsaken the commands of its God. They ask me for just decisions and seem eager for God to come near them. "Why have we fasted," they say, "and you have not seen it? Why have we humbled ourselves, and you have not noticed?" Is not this the kind of fasting I have chosen [says the Lord]: to loose the chains of injustice and untie the cords of the yoke, to set the oppressed free and break every yoke? Is it not to share your food with the hungry and to provide the poor wanderer with shelter—when you see the naked, to clothe him, and not to turn away from your own flesh and blood?" (Isaiah 58:2–3,6–7)*
>
> *God longs to push back the pain through those who serve as his body, his hands and feet on earth. . . . The body is supposed to do its work. God's work. . . . But we hem and haw. This is ironic since so many of us fault him for allowing suffering to be*

*the world's status quo. (The quo wouldn't be so status if we got off
our duffs and followed his lead.)²*

I think Joni would like Sartre's question: "Where was man?"
But where am I? Where are you? Are we really doing all that we
can to alleviate the suffering of those around us? Jesus once told a
story about the coming Day of Judgment in which the Great King
says to a choice group of men and women:

*Come, you who are blessed by my Father; take your inheritance,
the kingdom prepared for you since the creation of the world. For
I was hungry and you gave me something to eat, I was thirsty and
you gave me something to drink, I was a stranger and you invited
me in, I needed clothes and you clothed me, I was sick and you
looked after me, I was in prison and you came to visit me. (Matthew 25:34-36).*

His audience is surprised by the King's words and seeks an
explanation. "Lord," they ask, "when did we see you hungry and
feed you, or thirsty and give you something to drink? When did we
see you a stranger and invite you in, or needing clothes and clothe
you? When did we see you sick or in prison and go to visit you?"
(Matthew 25:37–39)

And then the biggest surprise of all is revealed. "I tell you the
truth," says the King, "whatever you did for one of the least of
these brothers of mine, you did for me" (Matthew 25:40).

So my question for all of us is this: What are we doing for the
King?

WHAT MORE THAN WHY

When we find ourselves faced with personal tragedy, I think
that the sixteenth-century reformer Martin Luther has some good
advice for us. He said, "Faith does not ask why, but what."

That is, What are You trying to teach us, God? What shall we do
with this thing? For what shall we use this experience?

---

² Joni Eareckson Tada, *When God Weeps* (Grand Rapids, Mich.: Zondervan Pub-
lishing House, 1997), 111, 112.

The trouble with many "why" questions is that they often lead to defiance and blaming. I must tell you plainly that I detest the current therapies that claim "you have a right to be angry with God" when something goes wrong.

A *right* to be angry with God? A *right* to shake your fist in the face of the One who graciously gave you your every breath and who lovingly served you every morsel you ever ate? A *right* to be angry with God? A despicable idea! Away with it forever!

Job suffered more than most of us ever will, yet do you hear bitterness in his voice as he cries out in agony, "Though he slay me, yet will I hope in him" (Job 13:15)? Paul endured more pain than most of us can imagine, yet where is the defiance in his cry, "I eagerly expect and hope that I will in no way be ashamed, but will have sufficient courage so that now as always Christ will be exalted in my body, whether by life or by death" (Philippians 1:20)? God can handle honesty—but who are we to rebuke God Almighty?

I never encourage people to express their anger toward God. Tell Him of your pain, yes. Plead for mercy, surely. Pour out your heart to Him, with all its disappointments and sorrows and agonies and all the rest—certainly! But the Bible never once hints that it's either morally right or psychologically helpful to throw a temper tantrum at the Lord. And the only person in Scripture who encouraged another to "curse God and die" (Job 2:9) is *not* presented as a model for Christian counseling.

When Job's wife gave this terrible advice to her husband, Job replied, "You are talking like a foolish woman. Shall we accept good from God, and not trouble?"

I refuse to accept the idea that people in pain should vent their anger at God. Still less do I endorse the current idea that we can "forgive" God, as though we were the judge and He the sinner! These are horrendous, even blasphemous ideas, and no counselor claiming to be Christian should ever espouse them. Rather, we should fall on our faces and say, "God, have mercy on me!"

It is true that many of the Psalms start out desperate—"Why, O God, have you forgotten me? Will you forget me forever? When will you come to my rescue?"—but they never descend into rage or bitterness. These writers are hurting, confused, weary, and even desperate, so they cry out in their great pain. And God never rebukes them for doing so! Yet it should also be noted that He seldom answers their questions. Instead He gives them Himself.

That is one reason I believe that a more helpful question than "Why?" is "What?" What do You want me to do, God? What am I to learn from this? What can I do to redeem this awful pain? It worked for Martin Luther, and it can work for you, too.

The Mystery of Suffering

I don't like suffering. I'm a coward and a chicken and in danger of becoming a miserable traitor to the cross when I start suffering. Yet sometimes suffering is directly on the path God requires us to walk.

There is deep mystery here. What does the apostle Paul mean when he writes, "It has been granted to you on behalf of Christ not only to believe on him, but also to suffer for him" (Philippians 1:29)? What does he mean, "granted"? In the original language the word is "gift." Suffering can be a *gift?* That's a mystery.

And what does he mean when he writes elsewhere, "I fill up in my flesh what is still lacking in regard to Christ's afflictions, for the sake of his body, which is the church" (Colossians 1:24)? We know that Jesus already did everything necessary to win our salvation by dying on the cross. So what could still be "lacking" in His afflictions? And how do we help "fill them up"? Another mystery.

Joni Tada, whom I quoted earlier, thinks that our sufferings (when handled in a godly way) may serve yet another function. She quotes Ephesians 3:10 and then writes, "Angels actually get emotionally charged up when people choose to trust in God. . . . God's purpose is to teach millions of unseen beings about himself; and we are . . . a blackboard upon which God is drawing lessons about himself for the benefit of angels and demons. God gets glory every time the spirit world learns how powerful his everlasting arms are in upholding the weak."[3]

Finally, I need to say that often the only time we think about God is when we suffer a tragedy. C. S. Lewis called pain "God's megaphone to a deaf world." In many cases perhaps tragedy is actually God's greatest expression of His love to you. Without the

---

[3] Tada, 107, 108.

suffering perhaps you never would have thought of Him. Perhaps you were so self-confident, so stubborn toward His love, so resistant to His call that the only way He could get your attention was through a tragedy.

Perhaps.

But none of us know that for sure. One day, however, it *is* certain that we who know Jesus Christ shall know even as we are known. The dark things will be made clear and the mysteries will be solved. I love the apostle Paul's statement about what's coming for those of us who know Christ: "I consider that our present sufferings are not worth comparing with the glory that will be revealed in us" (Romans 8:18). And the apostle's statement in 2 Timothy isn't bad either: "If we suffer, we shall also reign with him" (2 Timothy 2:12, KJV). Glory inside, reigning outside. Sounds pretty good to me.

LEAVE IT IN A JUST GOD'S HANDS

We live in a world gone awry, a world in which satisfying answers to troubling questions are not always easy (or even possible) to find. There will always be those heart-wrenching, soul-tearing cases that defy all our feeble attempts at "explanation."

What, then, do we do in such cases? Should we stand silent in forlorn resignation, hoping against hope that some good power really does reign in the universe—despite all evidence to the contrary? Or is there a better way?

About four thousand years ago a man of faith asked a question that reverberates through the centuries: "Will not the Judge of all the earth do right?" Abraham was deeply troubled by an imminent calamity he knew would take the lives of hundreds of men, women, boys and girls—and he wanted to be reassured that God, the Judge of all the earth, would indeed do right.

Abraham received that reassurance, and he walked away into the night fully convinced that God could be trusted—even though the threatened calamity fell the next morning.

Although Abraham did not understand all the ways of God, he did come to place his full trust in the character of God. He knew that the Judge of all the earth would do right. And he rested in that assurance, come what may.

That's how it is for all of us. There will always come a time (or more likely, times) when tragic events invade our lives, bearing no trace of God's purposes and no hint of rational explanation. What do we do in those times? The only thing we can do: We trust in the character of a loving God, a righteous God, a holy and compassionate God, who always does right.

A Lutheran pastor tortured for many years in a Communist prison cell in Romania tells an old story that helps us to see how God can be trusted even when it appears as if He has fallen asleep:

> *A legend says that Moses once sat near a well in meditation. A wayfarer stopped to drink from the well and when he did so his purse fell from his girdle into the sand. The man departed. Shortly afterwards another man passed near the well, saw the purse and picked it up. Later a third man stopped to assuage his thirst and went to sleep in the shadow of the well. Meanwhile, the first man had discovered that his purse was missing and assuming that he must have lost it at the well, returned, awoke the sleeper (who of course knew nothing) and demanded his money back. An argument followed, and irate, the first man slew the latter. Whereupon Moses said to God, "You see, therefore men do not believe you. There is too much evil and injustice in the world. Why should the first man have lost his purse and then become a murderer? Why should the second have gotten a purse full of gold without having worked for it? The third was completely innocent. Why was he slain?"*
>
> *God answered, "For once and only once, I will give you an explanation. I cannot do it at every step. The first man was a thief's son. The purse contained money stolen by his father from the father of the second man, who finding the purse found only what was due him. The third was a murderer whose crime had never been revealed and who received from the first the punishment he deserved. In the future believe that there is sense and righteousness in what transpires even when you do not understand."*[4]

---

[4] John Piper, *Living by Faith in Future Grace* (Sisters, Oreg.: Multnomah Publishers, 1995), 174–175.

I am not the slightest bit worried that when I get to heaven I will discover that God messed up. I cannot explain today why so many tragedies happen, but I do know that the Judge of all the earth always does right. Always. God makes no mistakes; He is absolutely righteous. The answer to Abraham's ancient question, "Will not the Judge of all the earth do right?" is still a resounding, "Yes, he will!"

I don't claim to know what goes on in God's mind. But I do know what He's revealed, and I rest in what I know of His character. I'm not more righteous than God, nor am I more loving than God. If God is God, He will not make any mistakes. Nor will He do the wrong thing or punish anyone unjustly.

Remember, it was Jesus who said, "If you, being evil, know how to give good gifts to your children, how much more will your father in heaven give good gifts to those who ask him?" (Matthew 7:7).

Our God is a good God, a righteous God, a loving God, an almighty God. He is a God who inhabits eternity, who sees the long-range perspective, the end from the beginning. He is moved by our suffering and concerned about our troubles, and that is why He sent His only Son to this earth to die on the cross for our sins to enable us, by faith, to live forever with Him in heaven.

This is a God we can love with all our heart, soul, mind, and body. We will not always understand His ways, but can always trust His character. That is the ultimate conviction that must sustain all of us, even when the answers we seek to life's tragedies escape our most searching gaze.

God *is* the Judge of all the earth, and He *will* always do right.

But I can't leave it there. As essential as it is to know and believe all this, it isn't enough. We must also submit our lives and our wills to God by placing our faith in His Son, Jesus Christ, who rose from the grave to win our salvation. God longs for a relationship with you. He is willing to give you answers to some of your questions, but He is eager to give you hope through a new life in Jesus. As Joni Tada writes, "Reasons reach the head, but relationships reach the soul. It's the friendship of God reaching out to us through our trials that draws the bottom line of suffering."[5]

---

[5] Tada, 126.

Remember Paul Little, the man I quoted earlier who was killed tragically in a car crash a quarter of a century ago? I still can't explain why God allowed his life to be snuffed out at such a young age, but I do know that Paul trusted in God with all his heart. As you read the following paragraph, remember that it was written by a man who is now enjoying the presence of the One he so loved and served:

> After we point out man's personal problem with evil we need to note that God has done everything necessary to meet the problem of evil. He not only came into human history in the Lord Jesus Christ, but He died to solve the problem of evil. Every individual who willingly responds receives His gift of love, grace, and forgiveness in Jesus Christ. As C. S. Lewis has observed, it is idle for us to speculate about the origin of evil. The problem we all face is the fact of evil. The only solution to the fact of evil is God's solution, Jesus Christ.[6]

What Paul wrote so many years ago is still true today. Jesus Christ is the only solution to the fact of evil. He invites you to trust Him, to give Him your life. And He invites you to do so today.

[6] Little, 72.

EPILOGUE

A VOICE FROM THE GRAVE

Many years ago when I was just getting my feet wet in ministry, I learned a crucial lesson from my mentor, the late Ray Stedman. As the pastor of a large and growing church, Ray was often called upon to offer counsel to men and women facing personal crisis. I never forgot one of his most potent warnings: "Woe to the man who has to learn principles at a time of crisis!"

Ray meant that the time to prepare for a crisis is long before it hits. It's too late to tie down the catamaran when a hurricane is ripping the shoreline. Therefore the wise person learns and internalizes time-tested principles of living while the sun is still shining and tragedy isn't rapping at the door.

I believe the best, most reliable and instructive principles of all are found in the Bible, God's Word. In this amazing book, the King of the Universe Himself gives us vital principles that will enable us not only to survive the storms of life, but to grow and even thrive through them. Here are some of the most important, but there are countless more:

God is a good God.
God makes no mistakes.
God is just and perfect.
God takes you seriously.
God gave Himself for you.
God keeps on serving you.
God has warned the human race of coming judgment.
God promises this isn't our final home; a better (or a worse)
one awaits.

All of these bedrock principles are taught in the Bible. And because biblical principles are true, they are trustworthy. The centuries have proven that those who live by biblical principles can weather any storm and can emerge from the fiercest winds triumphant and honestly praising God without forcing themselves to do so.

The Bible is also loaded with principles that tell us how we can manage our everyday lives to get the most out of each moment we breathe. The book of Proverbs is especially rich with these. Consider just five of its proven principles for successful living:

> Trust in the LORD with all your heart and lean not on your own understanding; in all your ways acknowledge him, and he will make your paths straight (Proverbs 3:5–6).
> How long will you lie there, you sluggard? When will you get up from your sleep? A little sleep, a little slumber, a little folding of the hands to rest—and poverty will come on you like a bandit and scarcity like an armed man (Proverbs 6:9–11).
> When words are many, sin is not absent, but he who holds his tongue is wise (Proverbs 10:19).
> He who walks with the wise grows wise, but a companion of fools suffers harm (Proverbs 13:20).
> When calamity comes, the wicked are brought down, but even in death the righteous have a refuge (Proverbs 14:32).

The Bible is a treasure chest of divine wisdom meant to instruct us in how to live well. So learn biblical principles day after day. You'll never regret it.

You can also learn principles from observing those who succeed—and from those who fail. Then make it your aim to mimic the former while avoiding the mistakes of the latter!

Why so much emphasis on principles? I believe that learning and applying such principles is crucial, for if you haven't suffered, you will. One of these days we're all going to suffer. So you'd better get ready! The question, of course, is *how?* What should you do if you want to be wise?

First, make a sound faith choice. Commit yourself to God through faith in His risen Son, Jesus Christ.

Second, learn how to grow in your new faith by regularly interacting with fellow believers in a church that honors Christ and faithfully teaches God's Word. Now, I must admit I've sometimes heard people balk at this point. "But they're just a bunch of hypocrites," they say. "Who needs them?" They simply don't want to align themselves with a local church.

And they do have a point. I know as well as anyone that churches are loaded with fallible people, some of whom are hypocrites (or worse). I'd never deny that; I've been in too many churches to say otherwise. But I *would* deny that it's a good reason to stay home and commune Sunday mornings with the Right Reverend Warm Sheets.

Let's be honest. *All* of us are fallible. *All* of us make mistakes. *All* of us occasionally act abominably toward others. We lie. We gossip. We look down on our "inferiors." We snub our rivals. Sometimes *we're* the biggest hypocrites around. But despite that, I have yet to hear anyone say, "Because I can be such a snob and a gossip and even a hypocrite, I strongly advise anyone with an iota of character to have nothing to do with me." The truth is, if we want to disassociate ourselves from all hypocrites, we'd better find a way—and quick!—to shed our own hypocritical skin.

Few of us, however, tend to think that way. Instead, we believe that we're pretty special, and all the hypocrites must congregate in churches we would never dream of attending.

Before we travel too far down that road, we should remember this: There are no perfect churches, just as there are no perfect people. I like what one Christian leader often says: "If you find the perfect church, don't join it, because you'll ruin it." We're all imperfect, and part of God's remedy for our sad condition prescribes close involvement with other imperfect Christians in the family of God known as the church. God states His case like this: "Let us consider how we may spur one another on toward love and good deeds. Let us not give up meeting together, as some are in the habit of doing, but let us encourage one another—and all the more as you see the Day approaching" (Hebrews 10:24–25).

Regular involvement in a Christ-centered church is vital to our growth in faith, but equally important is personal time spent in Bible study and prayer. There is no substitute for personally exploring God's Word on our own, and no alternative to personally directing our concerns and requests and praises to God's throne.

Think of it like this: We are eager to grow a strong, oaklike trust in God through faith in His Son, Jesus Christ. The soil in which the oak grows best is the church, the family of God. Bible study is the food that nourishes a healthy tree of faith. Prayer is the water that makes it possible to bring the oak to rich, green life. And God? He's the Sun that ultimately makes all of us grow!

But everything has to start with your decision to accept Christ's offer of eternal life. I urge you to discover God's extraordinary plan for you. Make your life count for more than just another birth and death notice in a local newspaper. You were meant for far more than that—and Jesus makes it all possible.

No matter what hurricanes are blowing in your life right now, no matter what tornadoes may one day hit you or your household, you *can* survive them and even thrive through them. But the only way to prepare adequately for the storms of life is to put your trust in the God of Abraham, the Judge of all the earth who *always* does right.

We never know when the next hurricane will hit. But *we can* know where to find the only anchor that can keep us safe through the whirlwind—no matter what kind of debris falls out of the sky. As one man of faith wrote many centuries ago:

> *Though the fig tree does not bud*
> > *and there are no grapes on the vines,*
> *though the olive crop fails*
> > *and the fields produce no food,*
> *though there are no sheep in the pen*
> > *and no cattle in the stalls,*
> *yet I will be joyful in God my Savior.*
>
> *The Sovereign LORD is my strength;*
> > *he makes my feet like the feet of a deer,*
> > *he enables me to go on the heights (Habakkuk 3:17–19).*

INDEX

NEW TESTAMENT

Matthew

Mark

Luke

John

Acts